Almanac
for Earthlings

elizabeth russell

EARTH DRAGON PRESS

The spirit of the story could smell the

danger, climbed down the clouds because

things had gone too far.

~ Joy Harjo

Dreamfruit 2023: Almanac for Earthlings

Copyright © 2022 by Elizabeth Russell

www.elizabethrussell.space

All rights reserved. No parts of this book may be reproduced in any form or by any means without permission in writing from the author.

Illustrations by Beth Lorio and Dan Reed Miller

Book design and layout by Ted Owen

Printed in the United States of America.

ISBN: 978-1-7342465-9-9

Earth Dragon Press

Eugene, Oregon

2022

What's Inside . . .

Welcome to Dreamfruit! You hold in your hands a uniquely enchanted almanac which is both a collective story and a personal moon journal, designed as a cosmic travel guide for the year ahead.

As a traveler through the Dreamfruit story, you are an earthling-in-training. Your mission is to wake from the **trance of estrangement** — that says humans are separate from the living planet — into the **dream of Earth**. This awakening brings you closer to your true identity, as an earth-being woven into the fabric of nature and the cosmos.

Now in its fourth year, the Dreamfruit story is told in the form of monthly missives from the moon Herself. As our benevolent witness and guide, Luna calls us to gather around the humming root of the World Tree. Throughout the year, she transmits a symbolic vision precisely calibrated to this pivotal earth-time. (Learn about the symbols that inform the Dreamfruit story on page 154 of the Compendium.)

Our annual pilgrimage consists of thirteen lunar cycles. Each New Moon adds a chapter to the story, like pearls on a string, revealing a collective dreamscape by way of prompts, reverie, and timely advice.

At the start of each moon-month, Dreamfruit travelers "enter the dream" for a magical briefing on current symbols and imaginal tasks. You may do this on your own, or meet with others in the sacred confines of the New Moon Café, a monthly virtual workshop and waystation. (Café dates are listed in the pages that follow.)

Then, bolstered by common cause, we embark on our personal journeys through the lunar cycle. We record Notes from the Field, visit the Altar of Mystery, and coax our dreams into fruition.

As with any good adventure, you'll be joined by Allies along the way. These allies may be strange or familiar, temporary or enduring, seen or unseen. You will find them in the pages of Dreamfruit, in your personal dreams, and in your day-to-day life. These friendly enchantments remind us that conscious agency pervades all of creation, and that the beyond-human world really does want our mission to succeed.

About Context and Imagination

You can use Dreamfruit as a lunar planner, a magical journal, a reference tool and more. Your way of relating to it will be as unique as you are. Whatever approach you take, Dreamfruit is designed to frame your personal journey within the context of the wider world. The journey is an eco-spiritual one, on course toward a viable and thriving Earth.

The world is at a crossroads. All at once, we are in a shared awareness of deep distress and resilient adaptation. Balancing the tension of these two truths can be challenging, and it's only natural to experience periods of eco-anxiety, overwhelm, or broken heartedness in the face of the changes we're tasked with.

At this very moment, your wild creative mind is home to a surprising remedy — a garden where story and dream wait like powerful sentries eager to be called into service. These forces sing deeply into the root of the World Tree.

Nature speaks to us through the deep imagination. What if we could remember this language and return to the matrix of belonging? What if the stories and symbols needed to teach us this language are spilling into the world as we speak?

To be clear, the deep imagination is practical and generative, a birthright tool. From it, we return with talismans, images, sensations, and a vision to guide us through daily life. Each year's story is a dream that bears fruit; a dreamfruit that can heal the rift between our broken hearts and the circle of life.

Yours on the journey,

As our story begins, the living Earth has been imperiled, and our creative nature is rising up.

*Remember! We are earthlings-in-training. The Dreamfruit mission is to return to radical belonging. Conscious connection with the living Earth is the natural state of earthlings, but in the rush and throng of modernity the ecological self can get left behind. **Here are the three key pathways to help you plot your course.***

Earthling 101

Magical Animism

Seeing the world around you as sentient will awaken your empathy and soften the distinctions between you and "other." Plants, stones, creatures, and even the written word can sparkle with mutual presence and agency.

Natural Time

Moving your mind out of linear time and into the flow of lunar cycles takes practice, but it is a surefire path to tuning into the larger cosmic intelligence. Inner states can synchronize with outer rhythms as we open to subtle cues from nature.

Deep Imagination

Symbols and dreams form a root communication tool between you and Nature, and can break through overly linear modes of perception. This inborn faculty can be applied with practical intent to discover new responses to the challenges of our time.

These three paths are woven into the structure and flow of the Dreamfruit almanac by way of these features: the monthly Allies (magical animism), Lunar Calendar (natural time), and the Dream itself (deep imagination). The How Dreamfruit Works section introduces these features, and greater depth can be found in the Compendium.

A Note About Astrology —

If astrology is not your thing, please don't worry that you are somehow missing something in Dreamfruit. I am an earthling whose languages include Nature, divination, dream, and more.

I've woven many modes of perception into the pages of this almanac, so taking an intuitive and experiential approach will provide you with the most fruitful journey.

For anyone, astrologer or not, a respectful apprenticeship to the planetary forces surrounding us can deepen a sense of belonging, and awaken a spirit of wonder. Astrology can be thought of as an intentional and embodied relationship to our cosmic landscape — one that reveals the archetypal "spirit of the time" and helps us find our best pathway through it.

Dreamfruit is not an aspectarian, but does aim to provide enough astrological information to help you trace the sky story. To that end, calendar data included are: the moon through its phases and signs, full and new moon degrees and times, eclipses, retrogrades, and planetary ingresses and stations. Seasonal themes are Northern Hemisphere, and dates are based on Pacific Time Zone.

Quick Start Guide

You can start right in by reading through the **How Dreamfruit Works** *section that begins on the next page,* **OR** *simply grab your favorite pen and . . .*

❧ **Go to page 12** *to get your "briefing" with the Story and Themes of 2023 . . .*

❧ **Turn to page 14** *to assess and create your own place in the story of the year . . .*

❧ **Go to page 16** *and write or place your guiding vision for the year in the Mandala of Belonging . . .*

❧ **Then, open to your first lunar month** *to begin the Dreamfruit journey!*

Now you're ready to step into the world of Dreamfruit 👉

How the Dreamfruit Almanac Works

The heart of Dreamfruit includes thirteen lunar months divided into seasons by color (blue for Winter, green for Spring, gold for Summer, and purple for Fall).

Each lunar cycle (or lunation) includes several pages of guiding messages, creative prompts, space for journaling, and moon-based calendar.

The underlying logic of the months goes from esoteric and collective (the opening dream) to personal and particular (the planning pages). This is the flow of "dream" into "fruit".

 On the new moon, read the Dream and let the symbols play in your imagination. Then find your ally, frame a seed question, and plant a dream-seed. Write, draw, or collage these into their corresponding spaces. As you become oriented to the themes, they will naturally emerge in your daily planning.

Now, onward to some of the landmarks you'll encounter on your journey through each lunar section . . .

1. Degree Symbols

Each monthly section begins with a special illustration from the richly gifted Beth Lorio. These thirteen drawings uniquely interpret the Sabian symbol for that month's New Moon degree. Visit page 154 of the Compendium to read about degree symbols, and let them inspire your deep imagination.

2. Allies

You will find an open "Ally circle" in each lunar section. Allies are here to impart an animistic and non-verbal layer of insight. Let these friends lend whimsy and support from the imaginal realm. The Ally circle is your space to record a word, symbol or image to serve as your personal ally for that month.

What or who is supporting you in your intentions at this time? Use a visioning process, draw an oracle card, or ask yourself what would feel most supportive in the month ahead. Invite an unseen or non-human guide to join you. Read more about allies on pages 17 and 166.

3. Dreams

Imagine yourself moving through Dreamfruit as a storied landscape, alive with its own cultural norms, characters, and magics. Each month's dream animates the current themes and gives the psyche a narrative of transformation. The monthly vignettes can be read as missives from a future being to help you conceive a pathway through the unique terrain of the time.

4. The Weave

The Weave speaks directly to the energy that might be pronounced at this time. These keynotes are informed by a range of esoteric disciplines, including the natural intelligence of seasonal shifts, astrology, and intuition. The *Weave* is our name for the unbroken web of life that moves within, between, and through all beings. When we slow down and listen, the Weave will surprise us with its benevolent wisdom and support.

5. Prompts

Notes from the Field are intended to guide you into inquiry and reflection. This is where you will find questions and prompts inspired by the energies of that particular lunar cycle. You can jot your responses here, take the prompt to your journal, or even bring it to a group process for deeper dialogue. We've made space here for you to record your own guiding question for the month as well.

6. Altar of Mystery

The *Altar of Mystery* is your space to bypass the rational mind and let symbols, dreams, and story step into the light and play. Write or draw with your nondominant hand. Collect and press images and leaves. Record a card reading. Build a paper shrine.

Of course, this is all offered in the open spirit of play and invitation. Please co-create with the pages and let this almanac become what you most need along the way.

Moon-Based Planning

The dated calendar for each lunation begins with the New Moon and is spread across four planning pages, with each page corresponding to one of the four main phases (or quarters) of the Moon. You can think of these as moon-weeks. Align your projects and activities with these quarters to embody the intelligence of their rhythm.

A deeper look at the moon's phases is included on page 158, but for our current purposes, here is the basic flow of each lunar cycle . . .

{ENVISION} at the new and waxing crescent. This is a time to identify your vision for that month and speak its name, even if only to yourself.

{ENRICH} with the first quarter and waxing gibbous. Nourish and cultivate the seed you've planted. Radiate energy and focus, and enjoy the momentum.

{SENSE} at the full and waning gibbous. This phase occurs in a variety of ways, from seeing your vision's fruition, putting the final pieces into place, or feeling the love.

{REAP} with the last quarter and waning crescent. Tie up any loose ends, cross the finish line, drop the story, and let yourself rest and reflect.

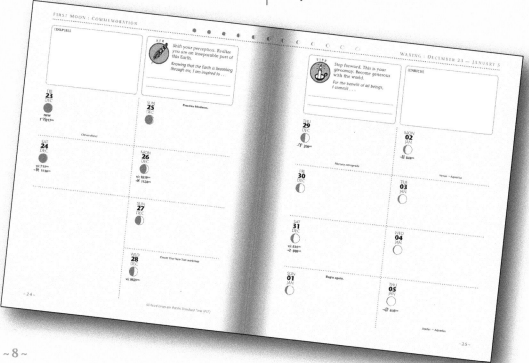

Each planning page is topped with two boxes. You can use the first box to record magical or mundane projects as they develop through each phase, use these spaces for a weekly oracle reading, or simply keep your lists here.

The second box indicates the elemental energy that correlates to that lunar phase. The open sentences found here are drawn from *The Work that Reconnects*. (Read in the Glossary about this approach to transforming ecological stress into heartful action.) Let these prompts guide you in walking the sacred circle through the energies of Air, Fire, Water, and Earth.

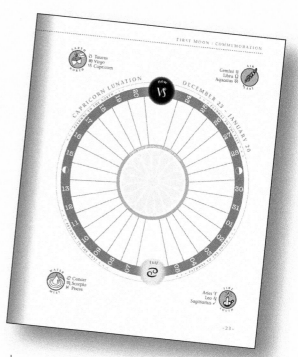

Moon Wheel

A special feature within Dreamfruit is the Moon Wheel, which depicts each entire lunation at a glance.

In the center of the wheel is a space to record the vision you are animating in the month ahead. *What dream-seed are you planting for yourself and the world?*

In each corner is an icon with a direction, its related astrological signs and elemental correspondences (Air, Fire, Water, Earth). You can refer to this key to start noticing the elemental energies at play each day.

The Compendium offers an in-depth discussion of elemental energies and some tips for working with the moon through the zodiac.

⭐ *The planning pages show the signs the moon passes through each day. Refer to the element icons around the Moon Wheel to find the sign's related element, and mark each day with a special color to track the energies of Air, Fire, Water, and Earth.*

And now, onto the path . . .

WHAT DREAM DO YOU CARRY THROUGH THE GATE?

I N THE LAND OF DREAMFRUIT *you will come upon a long silver coastline with morning mists and a sea-gray sunrise. There you see a small trust of women in scarlet robes walking the early morning waterline.*

Hear them sing as they step barefoot through the cold wet foam. They sing to the pebbles and bits of bone scattered like runes across the sand. They toss the song to and fro, each adding the next verse to create a living record of the dawn and the changes the night has brought to shore.

Dreamfruit is a call and response, a form of echolocation. It is how we know who and where we are in relation to the times at hand. It is how we measure the changes and read the runes — it is an augury, moon by moon.

The maps of this land tell us that a great fire breathes in the South, and the Eastern dawn brings light from the mind of creation. The waters of this land are vast and deep and clearly situated to the West, flowing and lapping against the chthonic shores to the North, home of ancestors and our winter lodge where we go to dream through the long night.

In the heart of this land, the World Tree reaches deeply into both Earth and Sky, and so the map also requires above and below.

Bow to the four directions, and to the earth below and the sky above. Feel yourself held in the circle of the world. Now breathe.

As you consider the terrain of the coming year, the unfolding story with all of its knowns and unknowns, give yourself a picture of the world you most want to walk within. Consider the days and months ahead as a tiny but consequential sliver in the span of geologic time.

And so, here we are gathered for the dawn of a new time. And we are stitching it fervently to the robes of Deep Time. A path appears, and we step through the gate together. 🪻

The Story and Themes of 2023

The journey this year is one of metamorphosis that brings you into radical honesty about what power and actions are yours to wield for the healing of your life and the world. As the seasons progress, we move from forest to between-lands to city hardscape. Imagine that you are spinning a glorious chrysalis, dissolving who you've known yourself to be, and emerging with a wildly renewed purpose. The journey changes you, and this year it brings a deep shift in identity and leadership, and renewed respect for how true power moves in the world. 🌿

Winter: Realization

We begin in the time of the three Winter Moons. We've returned to a familiar and sacred haven only to find it damaged by war. Our time here wakes us to the imperative of change—we contend with upheaval and loss, annul destructive contracts, and realize the range and limits of personal power.

This first season lays bare the stakes, rocks the very ground of who we imagine ourselves to be, and alerts us to the need to restore ourselves to the circle of life. All that follows is in service to this objective. Thus does a time of dissolution cross-fade into the quiet labor of soul tending.

Which internal resources come easily? Are there additional supports you can cultivate?

Spring: Reflection

The three Moons of Spring feel at once deliberate and strange. You sense a baseline shift, but it's not yet time to act. First, you'll need to re-constellate around a dawning awareness that you are not who you used to be. Be firm about what you intend to leave behind and what you mean to create anew. You've had a first taste of radical belonging, and now you lay the steady groundwork for its emergence.

While early Spring brings a soul-level awareness, you are soon called into gentle and ordered regulation of the ways power expresses through you. A time to gain practical skill, tend to the simple, and befriend your benign feral self.

Which practices help you feel patient and grounded?

Summer: Noble Summons

As Summer approaches, it's time to open to the unexpected, to discover previously unimagined possibilities for who you are and the unique role you fulfill in the ecosystem of your life and the world.

These months form the alembic—the alchemical vessel—for your shifting self-concept. Whether you readily embrace new identities or feel reluctant to relinquish the familiar, how you navigate these choice points will inform the balance of the journey. The Summer Moons bring you into the chrysalis, where your imaginal cells can do their mysterious work to shape your emerging identity.

What can help you refresh your sense of who you are?

Fall: Differentiation

In the time of the Fall Moons, the deeply internal discoveries of the prior seasons now bloom into a display of dignified glory. These months are your time to shine, but with clear eyes and firm ground.

As you incorporate the treasures from your time in the cocoon, new methods and identities arise that ignite spirited care and bold choices. Ready yourself to take a gentle but powerful stand. During this culminating season of the year, you're called to embrace your innocence, your unique perspective, and the heart of your leadership.

What do servant leadership and soft power look like to you?

Turning the Wheel

Although we learn a great deal about ourselves and make potent advances this year, the lessons of 2023 require more than insight. We must act with our newfound power for the benefit of all life. The Thirteenth Moon challenges us to step onto the Fool's Path. We may feel awkward at first, but a playful spirit will yield the most profound changes.

The Thirteenth Moon marks an ending and a beginning as the Wheel turns and a new solar cycle begins. The discoveries and challenges from the prior year don't go away; they enrich us with strength and wisdom as we step toward the adventure of the year to come.

Start where you are.

In Dreamfruit, we are continually dancing between the collective and the personal, the magical and the mundane. We've just discussed the Story and Themes of 2023. Now it's time to place yourself into the story. In light of the upcoming terrain, take a personal inventory of your gifts, challenges, and aspirations.

How do you most want to show up in the year ahead?

Gaze into this imaginary mirror and see an image of yourself as a Dreamfruit traveler — the hero moving through the terrain of the year.

Place a sketch, image, or word in the frame to represent the version of yourself that will be most helpful in 2023. It might help to first spend some time with the asset and challenge inventory below.

You might make a bookmark with this image so that you can keep your aspirational self in sight as you travel through the moons of Dreamfruit.

Gifts

What assets and strengths feel most available to you this year?

Challenges

Are there challenges you expect to face in the year ahead? List them.

If one of these gifts were a magical implement, what would it be?

For example: *My strength is seeing things from a wide perspective, so my magical implement would be a quill made from an eagle's feather.*

If these challenges could be contained by a protective vessel, what would it look like?

For example: *I am challenged by self-criticism, so I create a rose bush enclosure to keep my inner critic from running wild in my head.*

At the beginning of the new year, consider what you're completing and what you've gained during the prior year, and what you are ready to welcome into your life as you go forward. Use this worksheet to get clear about your values and supports.

Thank You 2022

What skills and insights have you gathered in the past year? Coming from gratitude can build a sense of strength & sufficiency.

Welcome 2023

What bright vision of the year ahead do you carry for yourself, for nature, and for humankind?

As you consider the year ahead, look over this list of words and circle any that stand out.

Power	Transition
Well-being	Luck
Ground	Self-Reliance
Discipline	Fertility
Love	Bridge
Adventure	Protection
Genius	Leadership
Refresh	Simplicity
Nest	Vitality
Triumph	Playfulness
Community	Ease
Instinct	Connection
Creativity	Service
Wilderness	Courage
Belonging	Honesty

Make your own list of words that name how you would most like to feel throughout the upcoming year.

_____

_____

_____

_____

_____

_____

_____

_____

_____

_____

_____

Your Mandala of Belonging: a circle of allies

Mandalas are a timeless technology of wholeness, a place for gathering your totality into the circle. There are thirteen lunations contained in this mandala, creating a map of your personal path through 2023. Follow the circle sunwise through the color-coded seasons as the sun waxes and wanes.

Your circle of support grows as you meet each moon's personal ally and place it here like a friend from the journey.

Finding allies

With each lunar month you're invited to identify a personal ally — a word, a being, or a symbol that helps you lock in the focus and theme you are tuning into most at that time. (Read all about allies in the Glossary!)

You will find a variety of methods can help in meeting this friend; oracle cards or writing can be helpful, and tracking synchronicities and your dreams will also give you clues. The ally may not become clear until you've explored the other prompts and messages within each monthly section.

Add as you go

The mandala becomes complete over the course of the year. Gather your allies into their corresponding moons on this page. By the end of the year you will have a full mandala that reflects your journey and the supports you've encountered along the way.

Make it your own

You can copy and use this mandala as a divinatory template for an oracle reading at the beginning of the year. Or perhaps you'd like to record a single card at the beginning of each month.

Begin again

At year's end you will find a simple meditation to draw all of these energies together into a single point of focus. This becomes a seed for the following year.

 To get started, find your personal north star by looking over your notes from the previous page to see if there is a phrase, word, or image that stands out.

What do you want to be guided or inspired by in the days to come?

Write, glue, or sketch this into the center of the mandala as a focus point for the year ahead.

THREE ROSE WINDOWS IN A GOTHIC CHURCH,
ONE DAMAGED BY WAR.

COMMEMORATION

{FIRST MOON}

CAPRICORN

The wound

is your

teacher.

IN THE DREAM OF THE COMMEMORATION MOON, *we begin with an ending. Eager to see the warm light stream again into the great halls, we turn toward the safe haven of our past.*

But the temple stands empty with shattered glass on its floor. What remains is still beautiful and carries great power, but the damage is evident. We cannot ignore it.

Within the singed walls we cast a bright circle. We carve a story of remembering into the stone. The story of the broken water and the brokenhearted. The story of the blind clutch of fear and division. We carve a warning and a wish, a burn and a balm.

And do we see the standing oaks? And are they our monument to life?

In the darkness, my love,
let us open the door.

When faced with serious danger, what is it that you seek to protect?

Name what has been lost — from your life and from the world. Create a soft place to hold their memory.

your guiding question for the month

write/draw/collage your ally here

As you begin 2023, take stock of past lessons and lay in psychospiritual provisions for the journey ahead. Turn to the Mandala of Belonging on page 16 to identify your seed syllable for the year ahead.

Don't forget what has wounded you, but give water to the green shoots that remain. Make a monument to what is most important in life so you can keep your values clear in the midst of hardship and change.

You can always go back, but it won't be what you remember. None of us is untouched by the world's love or cruelty. Post a warning at the gate.

Make an offering ❈ Consult the oracle ❈ Build a paper shrine

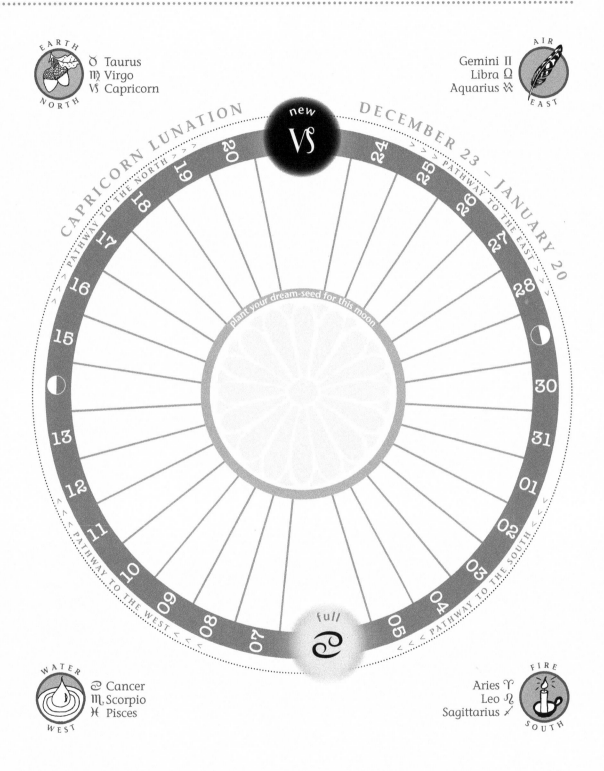

EARTH
NORTH
♉ Taurus
♍ Virgo
♑ Capricorn

AIR
EAST
Gemini Ⅱ
Libra ♎
Aquarius ♒

CAPRICORN LUNATION
DECEMBER 23 – JANUARY 20
PATHWAY TO THE NORTH > > >
PATHWAY TO THE EAST

new
♑

plant your dream-seed for this moon

20 19 18 17 16 15 13 12 11 10 09 08 07 05 04 03 02 01 31 30 28 27 26 25 24

full
♋

PATHWAY TO THE WEST
PATHWAY TO THE SOUTH

WATER
WEST
♋ Cancer
♏ Scorpio
♓ Pisces

FIRE
SOUTH
Aries ♈
Leo ♌
Sagittarius ♐

{ENVISION}

AIR

Shift your perception. Realize you are an inseparable part of this Earth.

Knowing that the Earth is breathing through me, I am inspired to . . .

_____

_____

Practice kindness.

FRI
23
DEC

Ⅴ

new
1°33' 2:17ᵃᵐ

Chiron direct

SAT
24
DEC

v/c 7:11ᵖᵐ
→♒ 11:14ᵖᵐ

SUN
25
DEC

MON
26
DEC

v/c 10:19ᵃᵐ
→♓ 11:34ᵖᵐ

TUE
27
DEC

WED
28
DEC

v/c 10:21ᵖᵐ

All listed times are Pacific Standard Time (PST)

FIRE

Step forward. This is your giveaway. Become generous with the world.

So that the world may flourish, I am willing to . . .

_____

_____

{ENRICH}

THU
29
DEC

→♈ 2:36ᵃᵐ

Mercury retrograde

FRI
30
DEC

SAT
31
DEC

v/c 4:44ᵃᵐ
→♉ 9:08ᵃᵐ

SUN
01
JAN

Begin again.

MON
02
JAN

v/c 2:16ᵖᵐ
→♊ 6:44ᵖᵐ

Venus → Aquarius

TUE
03
JAN

WED
04
JAN

v/c 4:08ᵖᵐ

THU
05
JAN

→♋ 6:15ᵃᵐ

{SENSE}

WATER

Honor your love and your grief for the world. Create space for your feelings.

What is difficult to witness at this time is . . .

_____

_____

FRI
06
JAN
full
16°22' 3:08ᵖᵐ

SAT
07
JAN
Create Your New Year virtual workshop
v/c 2:23ᵖᵐ
→♌ 6:40ᵖᵐ

SUN
08
JAN

MON
09
JAN
v/c 5:52ᵖᵐ

TUE
10
JAN
→♍ 7:15ᵃᵐ

WED
11
JAN

THU
12
JAN
v/c 3:06ᵖᵐ
→♎ 6:57ᵖᵐ
Mars direct

FRI
13
JAN

All listed times are Pacific Standard Time (PST)

E A R T H

Send roots into Earth.
Find strength in the gifts you
have already received.

*What makes me grateful to be
alive at this time on Earth is . . .*

_____

_____

{REAP}

SAT
14
JAN

WED
18
JAN

Mercury direct

SUN
15
JAN

v/c 12:40ᵃᵐ
→♏ 4:09ᵃᵐ

THU
19
JAN

v/c 2:09ᵃᵐ
→♑ 11:11ᵃᵐ

MON
16
JAN

FRI
20
JAN

Sun → Aquarius

TUE
17
JAN

v/c 6:27ᵃᵐ
→♐ 9:33ᵃᵐ

*"The stories that we tell about
ourselves and our place in the world
are the raw materials from which we
build our existence."*

~ Kendra Pierre-Louis

AN UNEXPECTED THUNDERSTORM.

AWAKENING

{SECOND MOON}

AQUARIUS

The change is upon you.

I N THE DREAM OF THE AWAKENING MOON, *even as we attempt to repair our paltry shelter, a fierce glowing storm descends.*

Under the elemental force, our temple walls slowly dissolve – first, into a paper-thin membrane of protection, and then into a vast canopy of trees cradling us as we cling to them for shelter.

We are pitched by the winds as they gust with blunt force. We hear the trees as elders, they whisper "Be rooted like us, be centered and soft." We release to the rock and sway of limbs, and a calm settles within our bodies.

And do our bones become branches? And does the flashing storm set us free?

Yes. The wild mystery is at hand.

*What is your
response to feeling
a loss of control?
Update your strategy
as needed.*

*Who can you
learn and practice
interdependence
with?*

your guiding question for the month

write/draw/collage your ally here

Prepare for the unexpected and remain flexible. Watch how birds and trees dance with the wind. Difficulty and chaos can widen your perspective and bring you closer to the spirit of nature.

The systems we've created to "protect" us from Gaia's unpredictability are now revealed as fragile. The gift of crisis is that it's a wakeup call. Like a brisk wind, challenges can be exhilarating.

Come together to give shelter and shore up resiliency. Adopt optimistic perseverance over vague foreboding. Tend to what is within your control, and adapt to what is not.

Make an offering ❀ Consult the oracle ❀ Build a paper shrine

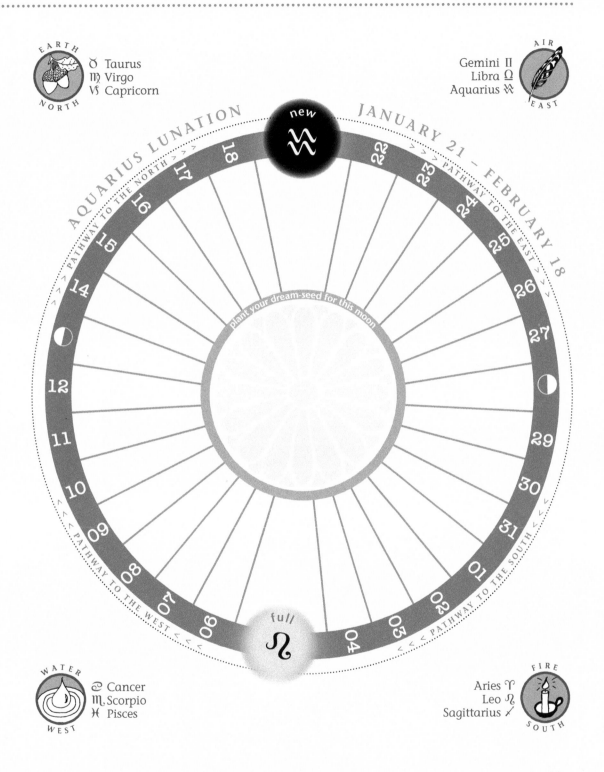

EARTH
NORTH
♉ Taurus
♍ Virgo
♑ Capricorn

AIR
EAST
Gemini ♊
Libra ♎
Aquarius ♒

AQUARIUS LUNATION

new ♒

JANUARY 21 – FEBRUARY 18

PATHWAY TO THE NORTH > > >

PATHWAY TO THE EAST > > >

18
17
16
15
14
12
11
10
09
08
07
06

22
23
24
25
26
27
29
30
31
01
02
03
04

plant your dream-seed for this moon

PATHWAY TO THE WEST < < <

PATHWAY TO THE SOUTH < < <

full ♌

WATER
WEST
♋ Cancer
♏ Scorpio
♓ Pisces

FIRE
SOUTH
Aries ♈
Leo ♌
Sagittarius ♐

~ 33 ~

{ENVISION}

A I R

Shift your perception. Realize you are an inseparable part of this Earth.

Knowing that the Earth is breathing through me, I am inspired to . . .

_____

_____

New Moon Café

SAT
21
JAN

v/c 7:52ᵃᵐ
→ ♒ 10:29ᵃᵐ
new
1°33' 12:53ᵖᵐ

SUN
22
JAN

Uranus direct

MON
23
JAN

v/c 2:19ᵃᵐ
→ ♓ 9:36ᵃᵐ

TUE
24
JAN

WED
25
JAN

v/c 8:12ᵃᵐ
→ ♈ 10:48ᵃᵐ

THU
26
JAN

Venus → Pisces

FRI
27
JAN

v/c 1:01ᵖᵐ
→ ♉ 3:42ᵖᵐ

All listed times are Pacific Standard Time (PST)

FIRE

Step forward. This is your giveaway. Become generous with the world.

So that the world may flourish, I am willing to . . .

_____

_____

{ENRICH}

SAT
28
JAN

SUN
29
JAN

v/c 9:52ᵖᵐ

MON
30
JAN

→ Ⅱ 12:35ᵃᵐ

TUE
31
JAN

WED
01
FEB

v/c 3:58ᵃᵐ
→ ♋ 12:11ᵖᵐ

Candlemas (Imbolc)

THU
02
FEB

FRI
03
FEB

v/c 10:19ᵖᵐ

SAT
04
FEB

→ ♌ 12:48ᵃᵐ

{SENSE}

WATER

Honor your love and your grief for the world. Create space for your feelings.

What is difficult to witness at this time is . . .

_____

_____

SUN
05
FEB

♌
full
16°41′ 10:29ᵃᵐ

THU
09
FEB

→ ♎ 12:47ᵃᵐ

MON
06
FEB

v/c 6:15ᵃᵐ
→ ♍ 1:14ᵖᵐ

FRI
10
FEB

TUE
07
FEB

SAT
11
FEB

v/c 8:41ᵃᵐ
→ ♏ 10:34ᵃᵐ

Mercury → Aquarius

WED
08
FEB

v/c 10:40ᵖᵐ

SUN
12
FEB

All listed times are Pacific Standard Time (PST)

EARTH

Send roots into Earth.
Find strength in the gifts you
have already received.

*What makes me grateful to be
alive at this time on Earth is . . .*

_____

_____

{REAP}

MON
13
FEB

v/c 3:52ᴾᴹ
→ ♐ 5:31ᴾᴹ

TUE
14
FEB

V-Day

WED
15
FEB

v/c 5:06ᴾᴹ
→ ♑ 9:00ᴾᴹ

THU
16
FEB

FRI
17
FEB

v/c 8:18ᴾᴹ
→ ♒ 9:35ᴾᴹ

SAT
18
FEB

New Moon Café

Sun → Pisces

*"If we are to avoid the worst. . . we
must cultivate and amplify our Gaian
imagination. We must learn to see and
feel ourselves being imagined by Gaia,
and so be inspired to celebrate and
protect the entire Earth community."*

~ Sean Kelly

A SQUIRREL HIDING FROM HUNTERS.

PRUDENCE
{ T H I R D   M O O N }
P I S C E S

I**N THE DREAM OF THE PRUDENCE MOON,** *we rest near the trees with ears perked and tails flicking. A quake in the grass and small chirp alert us and we are quick to curl into tiny hollows of branch and stone, camouflaged in the canopy and floor of the forest.*

From between the fronds, a familiar sight to each of us — the one who has stalked our dreams for so long — now clambers over the rocky trail. We know it seeks to harm, yet it lumbers loudly along, its prey safely sheltered throughout the landscape.

From our vantage we can see the radiant force of life pulsing from creature to plant to soil to sky, a sparkling web of signals and connection. The true danger here is loss of belonging, power gone amok.

And do the humble grow in power? And will we direct it to restoring life?

Yes. Your listening will protect you.

Caution

is also

a strength.

*What can
help you come
to terms with your
inner hunter and
prey?*

*Become a keen
observer of the
world. What do your
instincts tell you?*

your guiding question for the month

write/draw/collage your ally here

The web connecting us is also a safety net. Trust the small woodland animal within you. Know when to listen and stay close to the ground. Nature is the home field advantage.

Power can be channeled for healing or it can run amok and endanger us all. Chant the names of the Dark Goddess to open the path of the sacred warrior.

Resist undue pressure to do things that carry real threat. Find your own courage and let it show as measured caution.

Make an offering ❀ Consult the oracle ❀ Build a paper shrine

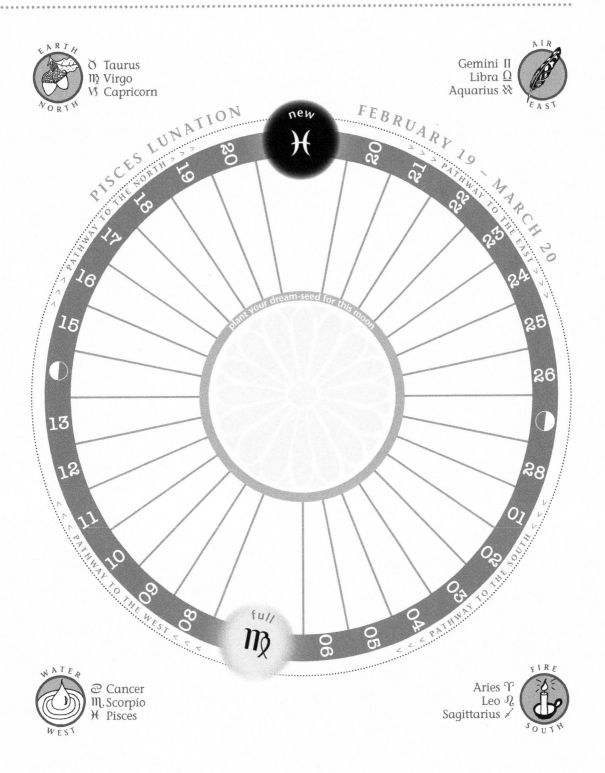

EARTH
NORTH
♉ Taurus
♍ Virgo
♑ Capricorn

AIR
EAST
Gemini ♊
Libra ♎
Aquarius ♒

PISCES LUNATION
FEBRUARY 19 – MARCH 20

PATHWAY TO THE NORTH >>>
PATHWAY TO THE EAST

new ♓

20 19 18 17 16 15 13 12 11 10 09 08

20 21 22 23 24 25 26 28 01 02 03 04 05 06

plant your dream-seed for this moon

PATHWAY TO THE WEST
PATHWAY TO THE SOUTH

full ♍

WATER
WEST
♋ Cancer
♏ Scorpio
♓ Pisces

FIRE
SOUTH
Aries ♈
Leo ♌
Sagittarius ♐

{ENVISION}

AIR

Shift your perception. Realize you are an inseparable part of this Earth.

Knowing that the Earth is breathing through me, I am inspired to . . .

_____

_____

SUN
19
FEB

♓

v/c 6:00ᵖᵐ
→ ♓ 8:56ᵖᵐ
new
1°22' 11:06ᵖᵐ

Venus → Aries

THU
23
FEB

v/c 11:22ᵖᵐ

MON
20
FEB

FRI
24
FEB

→ ♉ 12:29ᵃᵐ

TUE
21
FEB

v/c 8:06ᵖᵐ
→ ♈ 9:14ᵖᵐ

SAT
25
FEB

WED
22
FEB

SUN
26
FEB

v/c 6:42ᵃᵐ
→ ♊ 7:48ᵃᵐ

All listed times are Pacific Standard Time (PST)

FIRE

Step forward. This is your giveaway. Become generous with the world.

So that the world may flourish, I am willing to . . .

_____

_____

{ENRICH}

MON
27
FEB

FRI
03
MAR

v/c 6:22ᵃᵐ
→ ♌ 7:16ᵃᵐ

TUE
28
FEB

v/c 5:07ᵖᵐ
→ ♋ 6:40ᵖᵐ

SAT
04
MAR

March forth!

WED
01
MAR

SUN
05
MAR

v/c 7:18ᵖᵐ
→ ♍ 7:38ᵖᵐ

THU
02
MAR

MON
06
MAR

Mercury → Pisces

{SENSE}

WATER

Honor your love and your grief for the world. Create space for your feelings.

What is difficult to witness at this time is . . .

TUE
07
MAR

♍

full
16°40'4:40ᵃᵐ

Saturn → Pisces

WED
08
MAR

International Women's Day

v/c 6:07ᵃᵐ
→ ♎ 6:44ᵃᵐ

THU
09
MAR

FRI
10
MAR

v/c 3:37ᵖᵐ
→ ♏ 4:06ᵖᵐ

SAT
11
MAR

SUN
12
MAR

Daylight Saving Time begins

v/c 11:58ᵖᵐ

"We should take care so that we will lose none of the jewels of our soul. . . We need everybody and all that we are."

~ June Jordan

MON
13
MAR

→ ♐ 12:21ᵃᵐ

Pacific Standard Time (PST) becomes Pacific Daylight Time (PDT)

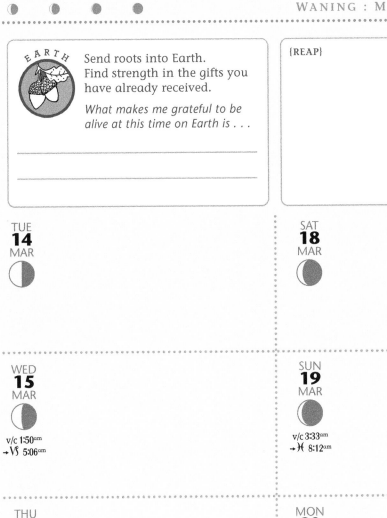

EARTH

Send roots into Earth.
Find strength in the gifts you
have already received.

*What makes me grateful to be
alive at this time on Earth is . . .*

{REAP}

New Moon Café

TUE
14
MAR

SAT
18
MAR

Mercury → Aries

WED
15
MAR

v/c 1:50ᵃᵐ
→ ♑ 5:06ᵃᵐ

SUN
19
MAR

v/c 3:33ᵃᵐ
→ ♓ 8:12ᵃᵐ

Spring Equinox

THU
16
MAR

MON
20
MAR

Venus → Taurus

Sun → Aries

FRI
17
MAR

v/c 7:14ᵃᵐ
→ ♒ 7:25ᵃᵐ

A WOMAN JUST RISEN FROM THE SEA.

A SEAL IS EMBRACING HER.

CHIMERA
{FOURTH MOON}
ARIES

Let awe

be your

companion.

IN THE DREAM OF THE CHIMERA MOON, *the winds have calmed and hunters have passed. The critterfolk show their faces, emerging from behind moss-covered boulders and poking between fern fronds.*

Then She rises, a woman or a seal or a shining drop of water from the sea. We encircle her, giving witness to this strange birth and the swirling bond between woman and water and wildling.

As the new hybrid emerges, a hush of wonder envelops us like the birth caul still clinging to her body.

And do we clear a path as She steps among us? And are we the fervent midwives of the earthling future?

Yes. The sacred depths give rise to multitudes.

*Play
with unusual
combinations. What
new creature can
you imagine?*

*Do you
remember how all of
creation shook when you
arrived in the world?
Tell the story or
make one up.*

your guiding question for the month

write/draw/collage your ally here

Watch for early glimmerings of your earthling nature. Your unique place and potential in the world begins to reveal itself like a luminescent pebble freshly washed by the waves.

Quiet your mind and don't be too hasty to find answers. Your dreams and the deep unconscious may stir new clues to the surface.

Your power called. It wants to be honed and directed for the greatest good. With Saturn now in Pisces, you begin to give shape to a dream through methodical effort.

Make an offering ❈ Consult the oracle ❈ Build a paper shrine

EARTH
NORTH

♉ Taurus
♍ Virgo
♑ Capricorn

AIR
EAST

Gemini ♊
Libra ♎
Aquarius ♒

ARIES LUNATION

MARCH 21 – APRIL 18

PATHWAY TO THE NORTH >>>

PATHWAY TO THE EAST >>>

new
♈

18
17
16
15
14
12
11
10
09
08
07
06

22
23
24
25
26
27
29
30
31
01
02
03
04

plant your dream-seed for this moon

PATHWAY TO THE WEST <<<

PATHWAY TO THE SOUTH <<<

full
♎

WATER
WEST

♋ Cancer
♏ Scorpio
♓ Pisces

FIRE
SOUTH

Aries ♈
Leo ♌
Sagittarius ♐

{ENVISION}

AIR

Shift your perception. Realize you are an inseparable part of this Earth.

Knowing that the Earth is breathing through me, I am inspired to . . .

_____

_____

TUE
21
MAR

v/c 8:58ᵃᵐ
→♈ 9:01ᵃᵐ
new
0°50' 10:23ᵃᵐ

WED
22
MAR

THU
23
MAR

v/c 10:13ᵃᵐ
→♉ 11:42ᵃᵐ

Pluto → Aquarius

FRI
24
MAR

SAT
25
MAR

v/c 9:19ᵃᵐ
→Ⅱ 5:42ᵖᵐ

Mars → Cancer

SUN
26
MAR

MON
27
MAR

v/c 6:39ᵖᵐ

"The universe seems to be the fulfillment of something so highly imaginative and so overwhelming that it must have been dreamed into existence."

~ Thomas Berry

All listed times are Pacific Daylight Time (PDT)

FIRE

Step forward. This is your giveaway. Become generous with the world.

So that the world may flourish, I am willing to . . .

_____

_____

{ENRICH}

TUE
28
MAR

→ ♋ 3:22ᵃᵐ

All Fools' Day

SAT
01
APR

v/c 11:03ᵖᵐ

WED
29
MAR

SUN
02
APR

→ ♍ 3:57ᵃᵐ

THU
30
MAR

v/c 6:45ᵃᵐ
→ ♌ 3:31ᵖᵐ

MON
03
APR

Mercury → Taurus

FRI
31
MAR

TUE
04
APR

v/c 6:50ᵃᵐ
→ ♎ 2:51ᵖᵐ

{SENSE}

W A T E R

Honor your love and your grief for the world. Create space for your feelings.

What is difficult to witness at this time is . . .

_____

_____

WED
05
APR
Ω
full
16°07' 9:34ᵖᵐ

THU
06
APR
v/c 5:43ᵃᵐ
→ ♏ 11:29ᵖᵐ

FRI
07
APR

SAT
08
APR

SUN
09
APR
v/c 2:09ᵃᵐ
→ ♐ 5:57ᵃᵐ

MON
10
APR

Venus → Gemini

TUE
11
APR
v/c 3:48ᵃᵐ
→ ♑ 10:33ᵃᵐ

WED
12
APR

All listed times are Pacific Daylight Time (PDT)

Send roots into Earth.
Find strength in the gifts you
have already received.

*What makes me grateful to be
alive at this time on Earth is . . .*

{REAP}

International Dark Sky Week begins

THU
13
APR

v/c 7:14ᵃᵐ
→ ♒ 1:42ᵖᵐ

MON
17
APR

v/c 11:57ᵃᵐ
→ ♈ 6:09ᵖᵐ

FRI
14
APR

TUE
18
APR

New Moon Café

SAT
15
APR

v/c 8:16ᵃᵐ
→ ♓ 3:57ᵖᵐ

SUN
16
APR

A DUCK POND AND ITS BROOD.

ENCIRCLING
{ FIFTH MOON }
ARIES

*I*N THE DREAM OF THE ENCIRCLING MOON, *an enchanted sleep comes over us and we are slowly absorbed into the vast surrounding shore. We root deep and deeper still into the silt and sand of the banks until we form a new membrane around a calm pond, teeming with life.*

We ourselves are filled with quiet assurance and a new resolve. We can feel it tingling in the soles of our feet and the pads of our hands. We become the nursery, holding circle in amniotic reflection while tiny but potent life dreams itself into being.

And do we remember the time before time? When the Great Mother birthed the world?

Yes. Tend the waters to support new life.

Rest

in the

ordinary.

What precious little things are you tending?

Observe tidepools and other watery edges. How can stillness foster new life?

your guiding question for the month

write/draw/collage your ally here

Training wheels are great! Learn to tread water in the kiddie pool before erupting into action.

No doubt you've stepped onto the path of the gentle warrior, but sometimes power is expressed in the incubation and protection of small things.

Hum mantras to your seedlings and embryonic visions. Review the choices and experiences that have brought you to this place, and bask in the liminal time between identities.

Pluto has entered Aquarius, unleashing a great trove of energy from the collective imagination.

Make an offering ✻ Consult the oracle ✻ Build a paper shrine

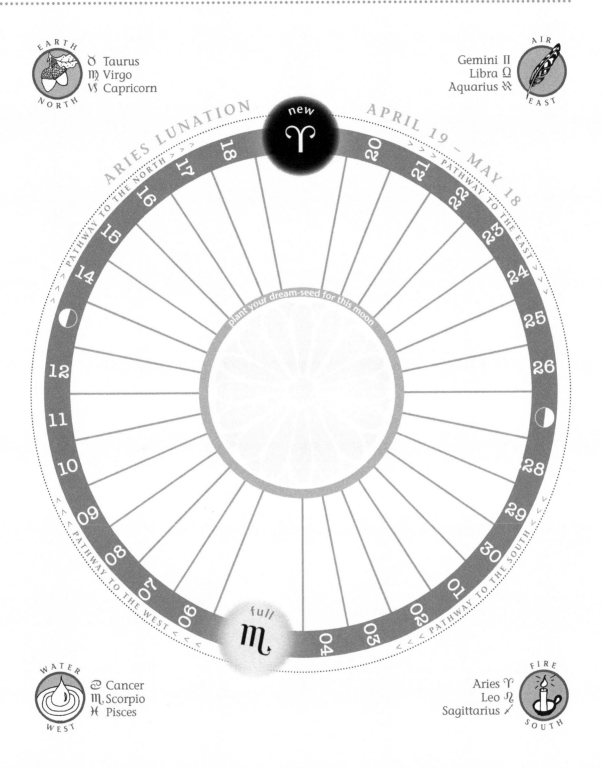

EARTH
NORTH
♉ Taurus
♍ Virgo
♑ Capricorn

AIR
EAST
Gemini ♊
Libra ♎
Aquarius ♒

ARIES LUNATION

APRIL 19 – MAY 18

PATHWAY TO THE NORTH >>>

PATHWAY TO THE EAST

new ♈

plant your dream-seed for this moon

18 17 16 15 14 12 11 10 09 08 07 06

20 21 22 23 24 25 26 28 29 30 01 02 03 04

PATHWAY TO THE WEST <<<

PATHWAY TO THE SOUTH <<<

full ♏

WATER
WEST
♋ Cancer
♏ Scorpio
♓ Pisces

FIRE
SOUTH
Aries ♈
Leo ♌
Sagittarius ♐

{ENVISION}

A I R

Shift your perception. Realize you are an inseparable part of this Earth.

Knowing that the Earth is breathing through me, I am inspired to . . .

_____

_____

Solar Eclipse

WED
19
APR

♈

new
29°50'9:13ᵖᵐ
→♉ 9:30ᵖᵐ

THU
20
APR

Sun → Taurus

FRI
21
APR

v/c 8:41ᵖᵐ

Mercury retrograde

Earth Day

SAT
22
APR

→♊ 3:11ᵃᵐ

SUN
23
APR

MON
24
APR

v/c 5:15ᵃᵐ
→♋ 11:58ᵃᵐ

TUE
25
APR

WED
26
APR

v/c 4:41ᵖᵐ
→♌ 11:30ᵖᵐ

All listed times are Pacific Daylight Time (PDT)

FIRE

Step forward. This is your giveaway. Become generous with the world.

So that the world may flourish, I am willing to . . .

{ENRICH}

THU
27
APR

FRI
28
APR

SAT
29
APR

v/c 3:53ᵃᵐ
→♍︎11:59ᵃᵐ

SUN
30
APR

Beltane

MON
01
MAY

v/c 4:53ᵖᵐ
→♎︎11:09ᵖᵐ

Pluto retrograde

TUE
02
MAY

WED
03
MAY

May the Fourth be with you.

THU
04
MAY

v/c 2:17ᵃᵐ
→♏︎ 7:32ᵃᵐ

{SENSE}

WATER

Honor your love and your grief for the world. Create space for your feelings.

What is difficult to witness at this time is . . .

_____

_____

Lunar Eclipse

FRI
05
MAY

♏

full
14°58' 10:34ᵃᵐ

MON
08
MAY

v/c 1:28ᵖᵐ
→♑ 4:33ᵖᵐ

SAT
06
MAY

v/c 7:38ᵃᵐ
→♐ 1:04ᵖᵐ

TUE
09
MAY

SUN
07
MAY

WED
10
MAY

v/c 4:52ᵖᵐ
→♒ 7:05ᵖᵐ

Venus → Cancer

"The deep dreaming of your psyche is one strand of the dreaming of the Earth."

~ Bill Plotkin

THU
11
MAY

All listed times are Pacific Daylight Time (PDT)

EARTH
Send roots into Earth.
Find strength in the gifts you
have already received.

*What makes me grateful to be
alive at this time on Earth is . . .*

{REAP}

FRI
12
MAY

v/c 8:15ᵖᵐ
→♓9:39ᵖᵐ

TUE
16
MAY

Jupiter ⤳ Taurus

SAT
13
MAY

WED
17
MAY

v/c 2:10ᵃᵐ
→♉ 5:28ᵃᵐ

Mother's Day

SUN
14
MAY

v/c 7:56ᵖᵐ

THU
18
MAY

Mercury direct

MON
15
MAY

→♈12:56ᵃᵐ

TWO COBBLERS WORKING AT A TABLE.

APPRENTICE
{ SIXTH MOON }
TAURUS

IN THE DREAM OF THE APPRENTICE MOON, *we dreamfast with the pond and its brood until we can no longer detect the thin seam between me, we, and other.*

The newly born spirit-of-place takes root within us. We can now hear the song of Earth. Indeed, we are each a humming strand within it — dreaming, breathing, and learning together.

This is how we discover a way to fashion soft slippers from the rootbark along the water's edge. We mold them to our feet and enchant them with remembering.

And do we weave a web even as we walk? And is it marked by our birthright bond?

Yes. Make a tether of your belonging.

Share

what you

know.

What magic tricks can you pass along to someone else?

Revisit or create a ritual that supports your embodied connection with earth.

your guiding question for the month

write/draw/collage your ally here

For a limited time, gateways
to ancient knowledge are
unusually discernible. Trace
your spiritual lineage to
identify and heal ancestral
land bonds.

The world may feel a bit shaky
this month. Become proficient
in your favorite grounding
technique. Make a sketch of
your earthling root system
and write up its operations
manual.

Listen to learn. Show what you
know to a respected colleague.

Make an offering ❁ Consult the oracle ❁ Build a paper shrine

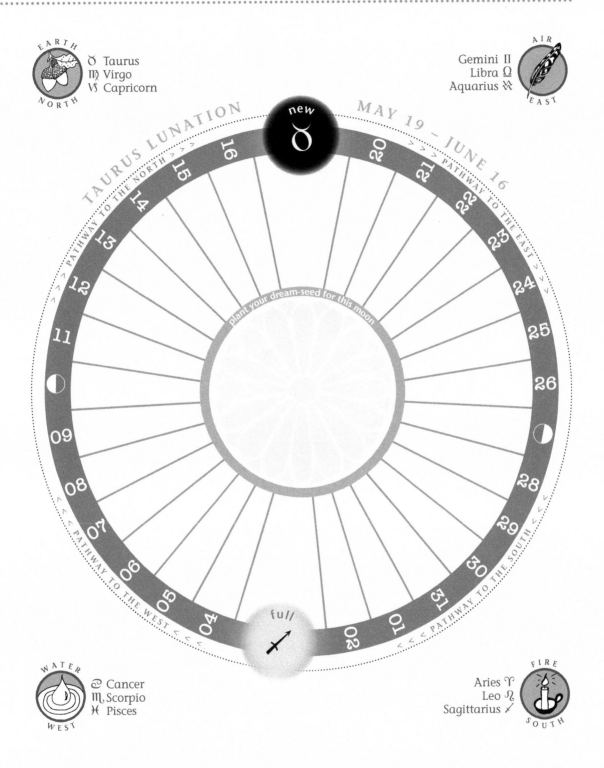

EARTH
NORTH
♉ Taurus
♍ Virgo
♑ Capricorn

AIR
EAST
Gemini ♊
Libra ♎
Aquarius ♒

TAURUS LUNATION

new
♉

MAY 19 – JUNE 16

PATHWAY TO THE NORTH > > >

PATHWAY TO THE EAST

16
15
14
13
12
11
09
08
07
06
05
04

20
21
22
23
24
25
26
28
29
30
31
02

plant your dream-seed for this moon

PATHWAY TO THE WEST < < <

PATHWAY TO THE SOUTH < < <

full
♐

WATER
WEST
♋ Cancer
♏ Scorpio
♓ Pisces

FIRE
SOUTH
Aries ♈
Leo ♌
Sagittarius ♐

{ENVISION}

A I R

Shift your perception. Realize you are an inseparable part of this Earth.

Knowing that the Earth is breathing through me, I am inspired to . . .

_____

_____

FRI
19
MAY

♉
new
28°25′ 8:53ᵃᵐ
v/c 10:51ᵃᵐ
→Ⅱ11:48ᵃᵐ

New Moon Café

SAT
20
MAY

Mars → Leo

SUN
21
MAY

v/c 3:12ᵖᵐ
→♋8:28ᵖᵐ

Sun → Gemini

MON
22
MAY

TUE
23
MAY

WED
24
MAY

v/c 2:12ᵃᵐ
→♌7:35ᵃᵐ

THU
25
MAY

v/c 11:38ᵖᵐ

FRI
26
MAY

→♍8:05ᵖᵐ

All listed times are Pacific Daylight Time (PDT)

FIRE

Step forward. This is your giveaway. Become generous with the world.

So that the world may flourish, I am willing to . . .

{ENRICH}

SAT
27
MAY

SUN
28
MAY

MON
29
MAY

v/c 2:46ᵃᵐ
→♎ 7:51ᵃᵐ

TUE
30
MAY

WED
31
MAY

v/c 7:53ᵃᵐ
→♏ 4:45ᵖᵐ

THU
01
JUN

FRI
02
JUN

v/c 5:51ᵖᵐ
→♐ 10:03ᵖᵐ

{SENSE}

WATER

Honor your love and your grief for the world. Create space for your feelings.

What is difficult to witness at this time is . . .

_____

_____

SAT
03
JUN

full
13°18' 8:42ᵖᵐ

SUN
04
JUN

v/c 8:24ᵖᵐ

MON
05
JUN

→ ♑12:31ᵃᵐ

Venus → Leo

TUE
06
JUN

v/c 9:40ᵖᵐ

WED
07
JUN

→ ♒1:42ᵃᵐ

THU
08
JUN

v/c 9:24ᵖᵐ

"Yet everyone is walking together,
all part of the story being
told again in a new way."

~ Stephanie Kazaa

FRI
09
JUN

→ ♓3:14ᵃᵐ

All listed times are Pacific Daylight Time (PDT)

E A R T H Send roots into Earth.
Find strength in the gifts you
have already received.

*What makes me grateful to be
alive at this time on Earth is . . .*

_____

_____

{REAP}

SAT
10
JUN

WED
14
JUN

SUN
11
JUN

→ ♈ 6:20ᵃᵐ

THU
15
JUN

v/c 6:36ᵖᵐ
→ ♊ 6:46ᵖᵐ

Pluto → Capricorn . Mercury → Gemini

MON
12
JUN

FRI
16
JUN

TUE
13
JUN

v/c 11:27ᵃᵐ
→ ♉ 11:31ᵃᵃ

A GYPSY EMERGING FROM THE FOREST WHEREIN HER TRIBE IS
ENCAMPED, GAZES AT FAR CITIES.

WILDLING
{SEVENTH MOON}
GEMINI

IN THE DREAM OF THE WILDLING MOON, *we emerge from dreams of water honey salt, moss root pond, to stand distinct — the earthling inside the human.*

We step away from the teeming cradle of the world, our slipper'd feet weaving patterns as we go. Spiral and labyrinth, circle and line, the path wends its way out from the nursery.

Our sensibilities are feral and we wake to the epic journey at hand. We're called to the distant hardscape, a city aching for the wild.

And are we earthlings, with birthright belonging intact? And do we hear the faint heart of civilization?

Yes. You are the wild emissary.

Greet

your

untamed

nature.

*How can
you be better
acquainted with
your inner wild
one?*

*What
do you see
beyond the edge
of your comfort
zone?*

your guiding question for the month

write/draw/collage your ally here

Your body is a multi-layered and untamed landscape dressed in the fashion of the day. Embark on a phase of cultural research and discovery. Gather somatic wisdom during these final moments of the Taurus North Node.

Your soul body is a willing agent of transformation for your social body. Declare your greater purpose and set your eyes on the path toward it.

What reminds you of your evolutionary inheritance? Study your hands, your soft eyes, your feet in the garden or the sand. Count your breaths and ask about the tiny and large organisms breathing with you. Greet the bright and unseen companions of your breathing body.

~81~

Make an offering ❄ Consult the oracle ❄ Build a paper shrine

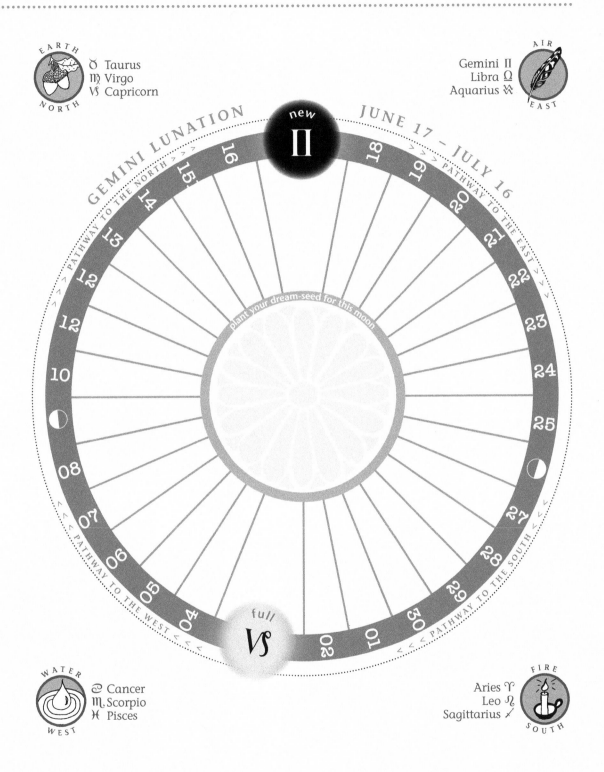

EARTH
NORTH
♉ Taurus
♍ Virgo
♑ Capricorn

AIR
EAST
Gemini ♊
Libra ♎
Aquarius ♒

GEMINI LUNATION
new
♊
JUNE 17 – JULY 16

PATHWAY TO THE NORTH >>>
PATHWAY TO THE EAST

plant your dream-seed for this moon

PATHWAY TO THE WEST <
PATHWAY TO THE SOUTH <<

full
♑

WATER
WEST
♋ Cancer
♏ Scorpio
♓ Pisces

FIRE
SOUTH
Aries ♈
Leo ♌
Sagittarius ♐

{ENVISION}

A I R

Shift your perception. Realize you are an inseparable part of this Earth.

Knowing that the Earth is breathing through me, I am inspired to . . .

_____

_____

New Moon Café

SAT
17
JUN

Ⅱ

new
26°43' 9:37ᵖᵐ
v/c 11:24ᵖᵐ

Saturn retrograde

SUN
18
JUN

→♋3:58ᵃᵐ

Juneteenth

MON
19
JUN

TUE
20
JUN

v/c 2:43ᵖᵐ
→♌3:04ᵖᵐ

Summer Solstice

WED
21
JUN

Sun → Cancer

THU
22
JUN

v/c 10:01ᵃᵐ

FRI
23
JUN

→♍3:35ᵃᵐ

SAT
24
JUN

All listed times are Pacific Daylight Time (PDT)

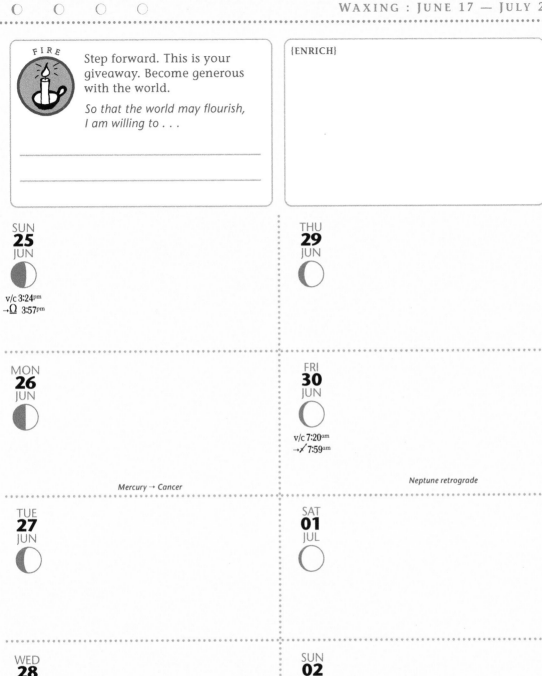

FIRE

Step forward. This is your giveaway. Become generous with the world.

So that the world may flourish, I am willing to . . .

{ENRICH}

SUN
25
JUN

v/c 3:24ᵖᵐ
→♎ 3:57ᵖᵐ

THU
29
JUN

MON
26
JUN

FRI
30
JUN

v/c 7:20ᵃᵐ
→♐ 7:59ᵃᵐ

Mercury → Cancer

Neptune retrograde

TUE
27
JUN

SAT
01
JUL

WED
28
JUN

v/c 1:19ᵃᵐ
→♏ 1:55ᵃᵐ

SUN
02
JUL

v/c 6:33ᵃᵐ
→♑ 10:20ᵃᵐ

{SENSE}

WATER

Honor your love and your grief for the world. Create space for your feelings.

What is difficult to witness at this time is . . .

_____

_____

MON
03
JUL

♑

full
11°19'4:39ᵃᵐ

WED
05
JUL

TUE
04
JUL

Interdependence Day

v/c 9:45ᵃᵐ
→ ♒ 10:30ᵃᵐ

THU
06
JUL

v/c 6:42ᵃᵐ
→ ♓ 10:33ᵃᵐ

"When we say the Okanagan word for ourselves, we are actually saying 'the ones who are dream and land together.' That is our original identity. Before anything else, we are the living, dreaming Earth pieces."

~ Jeanette Armstrong

FRI
07
JUL

SAT
08
JUL

v/c 11:22ᵃᵐ
→ ♈ 12:19ᵖᵐ

All listed times are Pacific Daylight Time (PDT)

E A R T H

Send roots into Earth.
Find strength in the gifts you
have already received.

*What makes me grateful to be
alive at this time on Earth is . . .*

_____

_____

{REAP}

SUN
09
JUL

THU
13
JUL

→ Ⅱ 12:26ᵃᵐ

MON
10
JUL

v/c 4:11ᵖᵐ
→ ♉ 4:55ᵖᵐ

Mars → Virgo . Mercury → Leo

FRI
14
JUL

TUE
11
JUL

SAT
15
JUL

v/c 5:35ᵃᵐ
→ ♋ 10:13ᵃᵐ

New Moon Café

WED
12
JUL

v/c 11:11ᵖᵐ

SUN
16
JUL

DARK SHADOW OR MANTLE THROWN SUDDENLY OVER THE RIGHT SHOULDER.

A WILLFUL MAN IS OVERSHADOWED BY A DESCENT OF SUPERIOR POWER.

THE CALLING
{ EIGHTH MOON }
CANCER

IN THE DREAM OF THE CALLING MOON, *we are on the edge of the wilderness and preparing to set off toward the hardscape beyond. First, though, we hold ceremony to proclaim our sacred assignment as we sing each other through the gateway.*

We step lively upon the path, singing "See me here! I am the ardent earthling arrived. The force of all life sings through me."

The Great Turning lays its claim on us and, with each step, dazzling feather'd leaves grow wide across our shoulders — a cloak, anointing us with deep purpose.

And does the power strike to the very fiber of us? And do we shine with Earthling dignity?

Yes. You are the glowing storm.

Let your

bright power

bloom.

*Declare
who or what
your dance is
intended to
serve.*

*What
beings do you
see living in accord
with their call? How
can that look for
you?*

your guiding question for the month

write/draw/collage your ally here

Briefly feel your gravitas
— your precisely ordained
purpose — then allow any
delusions of grandeur to burst.
Every earthling occupies a
humble place and purpose in
the grand scheme of things.

Create a rubric to sort calling
from career, but don't be quick
to know. There are multiple
stages in this metamorphosis.

The North Node's shift into
Aries is a clarion call to action.
Inject some swagger into your
steps. You are the Earth acting
on her own behalf.

Make an offering ❧ Consult the oracle ❧ Build a paper shrine

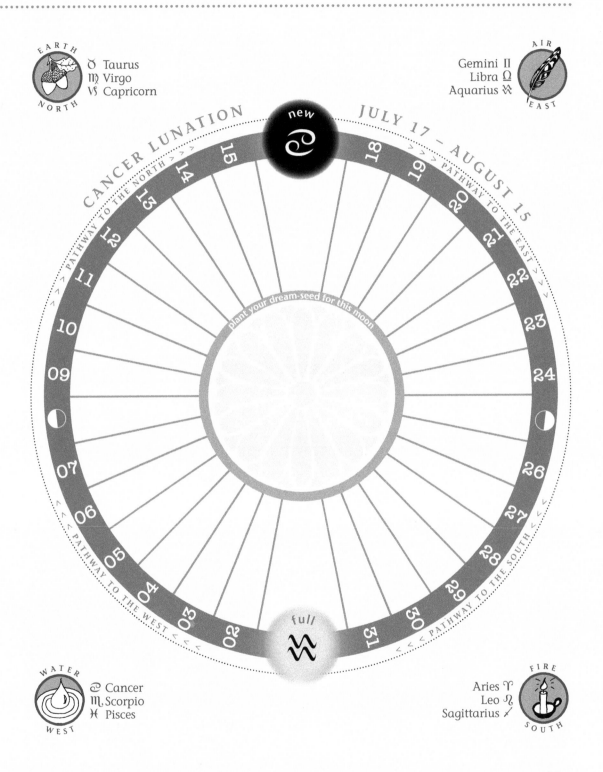

EARTH
NORTH
♉ Taurus
♍ Virgo
♑ Capricorn

Gemini ♊
Libra ♎
Aquarius ♒
AIR
EAST

CANCER LUNATION

new ♋

JULY 17 – AUGUST 15

PATHWAY TO THE NORTH >>>

PATHWAY TO THE EAST

15
14
13
12
11
10
09
07
06
05
04
03
02

18
19
20
21
22
23
24
26
27
28
29
30
31

plant your dream-seed for this moon

PATHWAY TO THE WEST <<<

PATHWAY TO THE SOUTH <<<

full ♒

WATER
WEST
♋ Cancer
♏ Scorpio
♓ Pisces

Aries ♈
Leo ♌
Sagittarius ♐
FIRE
SOUTH

{ENVISION}

A I R

Shift your perception. Realize you are an inseparable part of this Earth.

Knowing that the Earth is breathing through me, I am inspired to . . .

_____

_____

MON
17
JUL

new
24°56′11:32ᵃᵐ
v/c 8:06ᵖᵐ
→♌9:39ᵖᵐ

TUE
18
JUL

WED
19
JUL

THU
20
JUL

v/c 7:08ᵃᵐ
→♍10:13ᵃᵐ

FRI
21
JUL

SAT
22
JUL

v/c 9:06ᵖᵐ
→♎10:54ᵖᵐ

Venus retrograde . Sun → Leo

SUN
23
JUL

Chiron retrograde

MON
24
JUL

All listed times are Pacific Daylight Time (PDT)

FIRE

Step forward. This is your giveaway. Become generous with the world.

So that the world may flourish, I am willing to . . .

_____

_____

{ENRICH}

TUE
25
JUL

v/c 8:05ᵃᵐ
→♏︎9:55ᵃᵐ

WED
26
JUL

THU
27
JUL

v/c 3:36ᵖᵐ
→♐︎5:24ᵖᵐ

FRI
28
JUL

SAT
29
JUL

v/c 4:51ᵖᵐ
→♑︎8:44ᵖᵐ

SUN
30
JUL

MON
31
JUL

v/c 7:13ᵖᵐ
→♒︎8:58ᵖᵐ

Mercury → Virgo

{SENSE}

W A T E R

Honor your love and your grief for the world. Create space for your feelings.

What is difficult to witness at this time is . . .

_____

_____

Lammas

TUE
01
AUG

♒︎

full
9°16' 11:32ᵃᵐ

FRI
04
AUG

v/c 6:21ᵖᵐ
→ ♈︎ 8:19ᵖᵐ

WED
02
AUG

v/c 2:15ᵖᵐ
→ ♓︎ 8:05ᵖᵐ

SAT
05
AUG

THU
03
AUG

SUN
06
AUG

v/c 9:13ᵖᵐ
→ ♉︎ 11:25ᵖᵐ

"We are not divine, but we are the stable in which something divine is born."

~ Marie Louise von Franz

MON
07
AUG

All listed times are Pacific Daylight Time (PDT)

Send roots into Earth.
Find strength in the gifts you
have already received.

*What makes me grateful to be
alive at this time on Earth is . . .*

_____

_____

{REAP}

New Moon Café

TUE
08
AUG

SAT
12
AUG

WED
09
AUG

v/c 3:39ᵃᵐ
→ Ⅱ 6:05ᵃᵐ

SUN
13
AUG

THU
10
AUG

MON
14
AUG

v/c 12:46ᵃᵐ
→ ♌ 3:36ᵃᵐ

FRI
11
AUG

v/c 10:27ᵃᵐ
→ ♋ 3:52ᵖᵐ

TUE
15
AUG

AN UNTIDY, UNKEMPT MAN. TOTALLY CONCENTRATED UPON
INNER SPIRITUAL ATTAINMENT, A YOGI IS SITTING.

CHRYSALIS
{NINTH MOON}
LEO

I N THE DREAM OF THE CHRYSALIS MOON, *we are travelers heading toward what is called "the civilized places". We are in the between lands of* desert, crossing a bare landscape.

The hot sky burns the dross from our eyes and we take shade beneath our dazzling cloaks. We feel ourselves enfolded in a crucible as our mantles grow larger to encompass us.

Here in this solitary in-between, a molting process begins. We hum eccentrically to ourselves, oblivious within our shimmering cocoons.

And does the new skin grow just beneath the old? And must we remake old forms in order to fulfill our task?

Yes. The dreaming Earth will reshape you.

Go deep

to go

far.

*Create a
personal formula
for power. Fold-in
earthlove and insight
with equal
measure.*

*Is there
something you
must set aside in
order to serve a
deeper call?*

your guiding question for the month

write/draw/collage your ally here

Step into the wilderness and slip out of time. Get dirt on your skin and quiet in your heart. Concentrate on birdsong and bugtrails and grit and your animal body.

If you are lucky, you are beginning to sense a baseline shift in identity. Something new and strong is taking shape and needs your spiritual warriorship to usher it in.

Be willing to buck social norms in order to achieve a higher calling or goal. This is not a time to be distracted by superficial concerns. Let your freak light shine!

Make an offering ❄ Consult the oracle ❄ Build a paper shrine

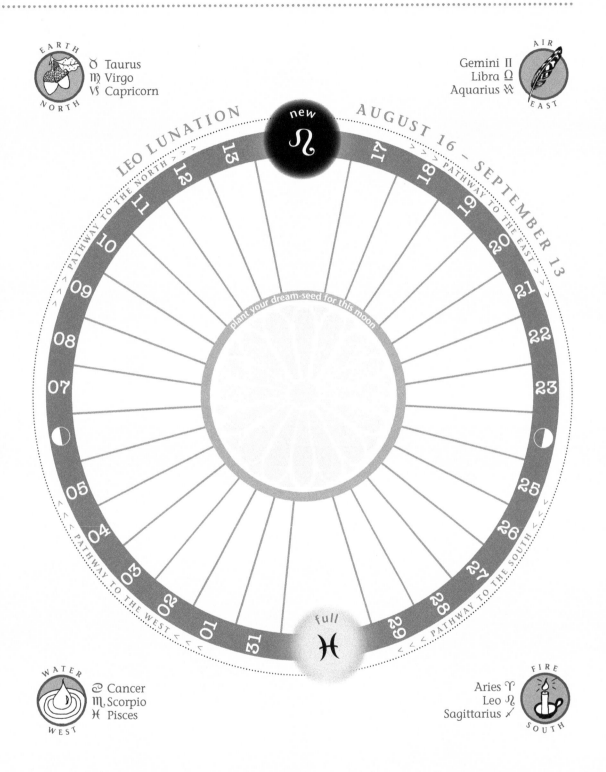

EARTH
NORTH
☿ Taurus
♍ Virgo
♑ Capricorn

AIR
EAST
Gemini ♊
Libra ♎
Aquarius ♒

LEO LUNATION

AUGUST 16 – SEPTEMBER 13

PATHWAY TO THE NORTH >>>

PATHWAY TO THE EAST

new ♌

13 12 11 10 09 08 07 05 04 03 02 01 31 29 28 27 26 25 23 22 21 20 19 18 17

plant your dream-seed for this moon

PATHWAY TO THE WEST <<<

PATHWAY TO THE SOUTH <<<

full ♓

WATER
WEST
♋ Cancer
♏ Scorpio
♓ Pisces

FIRE
SOUTH
Aries ♈
Leo ♌
Sagittarius ♐

~103~

{ENVISION}

AIR

Shift your perception. Realize you are an inseparable part of this Earth.

Knowing that the Earth is breathing through me, I am inspired to . . .

_____

_____

WED
16
AUG

new
23°17' 2:38ᵃᵐ
→♍4:14ᵖᵐ

THU
17
AUG

SUN
20
AUG

MON
21
AUG

v/c 1:31ᵖᵐ
→♏4:22ᵖᵐ

FRI
18
AUG

TUE
22
AUG

SAT
19
AUG

v/c 1:51ᵃᵐ
→♎4:53ᵃᵐ

WED
23
AUG

v/c 10:10ᵖᵐ

Sun → Virgo . Mercury retrograde

All listed times are Pacific Daylight Time (PDT)

FIRE

Step forward. This is your giveaway. Become generous with the world.

So that the world may flourish, I am willing to . . .

{ENRICH}

THU
24
AUG

⟶♐ 1:07ᵃᵐ

FRI
25
AUG

SAT
26
AUG

v/c 4:56ᵃᵐ
⟶♑ 6:05ᵃᵐ

SUN
27
AUG

Mars ⟶ Libra

MON
28
AUG

v/c 4:49ᵃᵐ
⟶♒ 7:32ᵃᵐ

Uranus retrograde

TUE
29
AUG

v/c 8:04ᵖᵐ

{SENSE}

WATER

Honor your love and your grief for the world. Create space for your feelings.

What is difficult to witness at this time is . . .

_____

_____

WED
30
AUG

♓

→ ♓ 6:56ᵃᵐ
full
7°25' 6:36ᵖᵐ

THU
31
AUG

FRI
01
SEP

v/c 3:36ᵃᵐ
→ ♈ 6:25ᵃᵐ

SAT
02
SEP

v/c 5:40ᵃᵐ
→ ♏ 8:45ᵃᵐ

SUN
03
SEP

v/c 4:57ᵃᵐ
→ ♉ 8:00ᵃᵐ

Venus direct

MON
04
SEP

Labor Day

Jupiter retrograde

TUE
05
SEP

v/c 9:46ᵃᵐ
→ ♊ 1:07ᵖᵐ

"We are all lives in other skins, furs, feathers, or scales, each with different visions and dreams and histories, different kinds of earth intelligence, all of it making for one great whole."

~ Linda Hogan

All listed times are Pacific Daylight Time (PDT)

EARTH

Send roots into Earth.
Find strength in the gifts you
have already received.

*What makes me grateful to be
alive at this time on Earth is . . .*

{REAP}

WED
06
SEP

SUN
10
SEP

v/c 5:47ᵃᵐ
→ ♌ 9:36ᵃᵐ

THU
07
SEP

v/c 3:22ᵖᵐ
→ ♋ 10:00ᵖᵐ

MON
11
SEP

FRI
08
SEP

TUE
12
SEP

v/c 8:06ᵃᵐ
→ ♍ 10:18ᵖᵐ

SAT
09
SEP

New Moon Café

WED
13
SEP

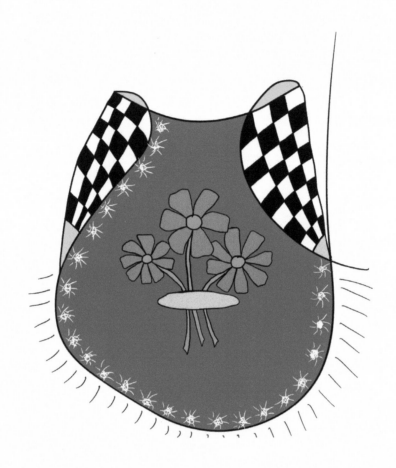

A ROYAL COAT OF ARMS ENRICHED WITH PRECIOUS STONES.

IMAGO
{ TENTH MOON }
VIRGO

Remember

who you

are.

IN THE DREAM OF THE IMAGO MOON, *our cocoons burst into brightly colored wings of leaf feather and bark. They briefly crystallize into a dazzling latticework that reads like a scroll telling the story of our origins and relationships, our deep belonging.*

The markings resolve into a brilliant cloak before shrinking even further into a shining talisman pressed into our chests. The clan to which we belong and that we are pledged to protect — wing fin fur claw the rooted ones the star beings river mountain cloud — all of our kin now claim us as their own.

A rush of relief and recognition as the final piece of an ancient puzzle at last clicks into place.

And do we awake from a long sorrow? And do we take the Earthling mark?

Yes. Awaken your creative nature.

Where do you come from? Look for traits in common with fish, tree, and sky.

You are filled with wonders unnamed. How do you picture your mythopoetic identity?

your guiding question for the month

write/draw/collage your ally here

Design and draw your Crest of Belonging. Let it convey what you stand for, your talents and your particular assignment.

Families of origin can sometimes feel chaotic or frayed. But there is a deeper inheritance at play. Seek out discernible patterns in your earth-lineage. Stabilize and "true the wheel", even through the mists of deep time.

Trace your roots and update the story you tell about where you come from. In the evolutionary journey, all heritage is noble. Make a proclamation on behalf of your kin.

Make an offering ❄ Consult the oracle ❄ Build a paper shrine

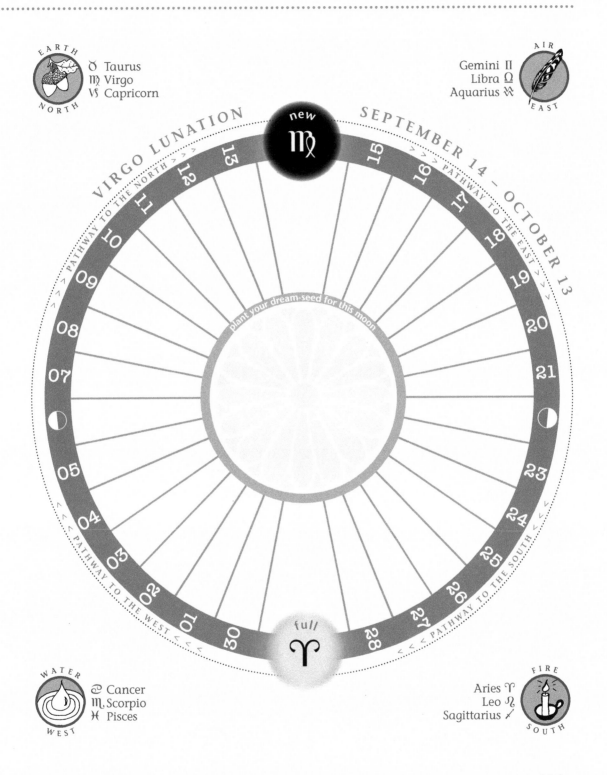

EARTH NORTH
♉ Taurus
♍ Virgo
♑ Capricorn

AIR EAST
Gemini ♊
Libra ♎
Aquarius ♒

VIRGO LUNATION

SEPTEMBER 14 – OCTOBER 13

new ♍

PATHWAY TO THE NORTH >>>

PATHWAY TO THE EAST >

plant your dream-seed for this moon

PATHWAY TO THE WEST <<<

PATHWAY TO THE SOUTH <<<

full ♈

13 12 11 10 09 08 07 05 04 03 02 01 30 28 27 26 25 24 23 21 20 19 18 17 16 15

WATER WEST
♋ Cancer
♏ Scorpio
♓ Pisces

FIRE SOUTH
Aries ♈
Leo ♌
Sagittarius ♐

{ENVISION}

Shift your perception. Realize you are an inseparable part of this Earth.

Knowing that the Earth is breathing through me, I am inspired to . . .

_____

_____

THU
14
SEP

new
21°59' 6:40ᵖᵐ

MON
18
SEP

FRI
15
SEP

v/c 6:49ᵃᵐ
→♎10:44ᵃᵐ

Mercury direct

TUE
19
SEP

SAT
16
SEP

WED
20
SEP

v/c 3:21ᵃᵐ
→♐7:06ᵃᵐ

SUN
17
SEP

v/c 6:06ᵖᵐ
→♏9:58ᵖᵐ

THU
21
SEP

International Day of Peace

All listed times are Pacific Daylight Time (PDT)

FIRE

Step forward. This is your giveaway. Become generous with the world.

So that the world may flourish, I am willing to . . .

{ENRICH}

Fall Equinox

FRI
22
SEP

v/c 12:32ᵖᵐ
→ ♑ 1:20ᵖᵐ

Sun → Libra

TUE
26
SEP

v/c 5:38ᵃᵐ
→ ♓ 5:18ᵖᵐ

SAT
23
SEP

WED
27
SEP

SUN
24
SEP

v/c 1:05ᵖᵐ
→ ♒ 4:29ᵖᵐ

THU
28
SEP

v/c 1:58ᵖᵐ
→ ♈ 5:17ᵖᵐ

MON
25
SEP

{SENSE}

WATER Honor your love and your grief for the world. Create space for your feelings.

What is difficult to witness at this time is . . .

_____

_____

FRI
29
SEP

♈

full
6°00' 2:58ᵃᵐ

SAT
30
SEP

v/c 2:50ᵖᵐ
→ ♉6:18ᵖᵐ

SUN
01
OCT

MON
02
OCT

v/c 6:20ᵖᵐ
→ ♊ 10:03ᵖᵐ

TUE
03
OCT

WED
04
OCT

v/c 11:34ᵖᵐ

Mercury → Libra

"We are living within this wider thing, the mundus imaginalis, *the soul of the world, and your dreams and your opinions are connected to waterfalls and jaguars and lightning storms."*

~ Martin Shaw

THU
05
OCT

→ ♋5:32ᵃᵐ

All listed times are Pacific Daylight Time (PDT)

E A R T H Send roots into Earth.
Find strength in the gifts you
have already received.

*What makes me grateful to be
alive at this time on Earth is . . .*

_____

_____

{REAP}

FRI
06
OCT

SAT
07
OCT

v/c 12:12ᵖᵐ
→ ♌ 4:24ᵖᵐ

SUN
08
OCT

Venus → Virgo

Indigenous Peoples' Day

MON
09
OCT

TUE
10
OCT

v/c 2:37ᵃᵐ
→ ♍ 5:02ᵃᵐ

Pluto direct

WED
11
OCT

Mars → Scorpio

THU
12
OCT

v/c 1:10ᵖᵐ
→ ♎ 5:22ᵖᵐ

FRI
13
OCT

A CHILD GIVING BIRDS A DRINK AT A FOUNTAIN.

COVENANT

{ ELEVENTH MOON }

LIBRA

Open a

channel.

IN THE DREAM OF THE COVENANT MOON, *we enter the hardscape of city only to find the birds have gone quiet and the trees are thirsty and bent. They lean toward us, having heard from the songs of their forest cousins and through the belowground network that we, the changed, are arriving.*

In search of water, we find the glorious river has been sequestered for human industry, diverted away from its sisters and brothers, flora and fauna.

The river herself mourns her separation, yearning to bring life again. We offer our human hands to join cause and stitch them back together.

And can we set the water free? And will it now flow toward life?

Yes. Great power seeks its noble cause.

*Place a fresh
water source in
your garden for the
creatures who pass
through.*

*What is
within your hands
to do? What has
been placed in
your care?*

your guiding question for the month

write/draw/collage your ally here

This is a watershed moment!
You're called to direct all of your
best resources to serve the earth
community. Here, in this modern
world, some part of us always
remembers no separation and
wants to give care.

Kindness itself is an inherent
virtue. After the deep growth
of the year, you arrive
at something simple but
profound. Actions feel like
natural action, inevitable
and healthy responses to a
situation of need.

Even in the built world,
humankind expresses its nature
bond. Much of our technology
has been or can be bent to
serve life. Find the servant
leaders in your community.

Make an offering ❧ Consult the oracle ❧ Build a paper shrine

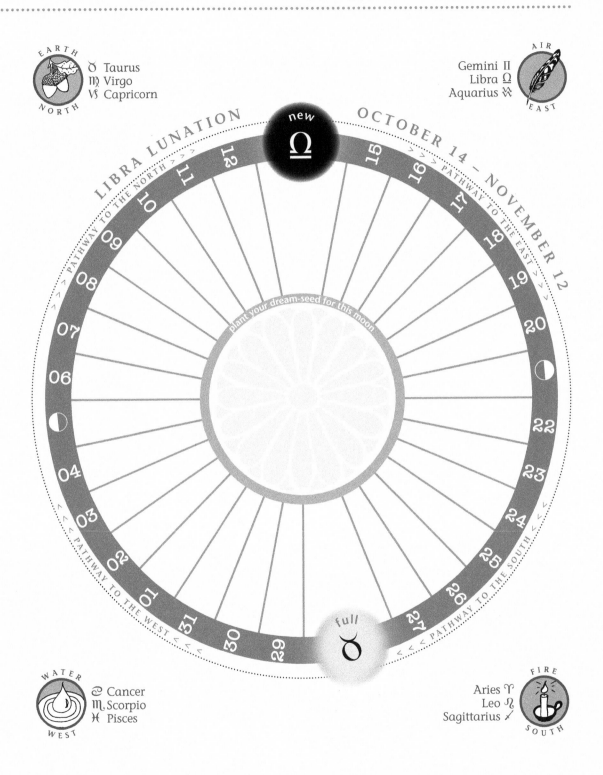

EARTH
NORTH
♉ Taurus
♍ Virgo
♑ Capricorn

AIR
EAST
Gemini ♊
Libra ♎
Aquarius ♒

new
♎

LIBRA LUNATION

OCTOBER 14 – NOVEMBER 12

PATHWAY TO THE NORTH > > >

PATHWAY TO THE EAST ∨ ∨

12
11
10
09
08
07
06
04
03
02
01
31
30
29

15
16
17
18
19
20
22
23
24
25
26
27

plant your dream-seed for this moon

PATHWAY TO THE WEST < < <

< < < PATHWAY TO THE SOUTH

full
♉

WATER
WEST
♋ Cancer
♏ Scorpio
♓ Pisces

FIRE
SOUTH
Aries ♈
Leo ♌
Sagittarius ♐

{ENVISION}

AIR

Shift your perception. Realize you are an inseparable part of this Earth.

Knowing that the Earth is breathing through me, I am inspired to . . .

_____

_____

Solar Eclipse . *New Moon Café*

SAT
14
OCT

Ω

new
21°08'10:55ᵃᵐ

SUN
15
OCT

v/c 12:01ᵃᵐ
→♏4:04ᵃᵐ

MON
16
OCT

TUE
17
OCT

v/c 8:44ᵃᵐ
→♐12:36ᵖᵐ

WED
18
OCT

THU
19
OCT

v/c 12:02ᵖᵐ
→♑6:55ᵖᵐ

FRI
20
OCT

"Compassion is the keen awareness of the interdependence of all things."

~ Thomas Merton

All listed times are Pacific Daylight Time (PDT)

FIRE

Step forward. This is your giveaway. Become generous with the world.

So that the world may flourish, I am willing to . . .

_____

_____

{ENRICH}

SAT
21
OCT

v/c 11:00pm
→♏︎11:06pm

Mercury → Scorpio

WED
25
OCT

v/c 11:39pm

SUN
22
OCT

THU
26
OCT

→♈︎3:02am

MON
23
OCT

v/c 12:04pm

Sun → Scorpio

FRI
27
OCT

TUE
24
OCT

→♓︎1:33am

{SENSE}

WATER

Honor your love and your grief for the world. Create space for your feelings.

What is difficult to witness at this time is . . .

_____

_____

Lunar Eclipse

SAT
28
OCT

♉

v/c 1:20ᵃᵐ
→ ♉ 4:44ᵃᵐ
full
5°09' 1:24ᵖᵐ

Day of the Dead

WED
01
NOV

v/c 5:36ᵃᵐ
→ ♋ 2:30ᵖᵐ

SUN
29
OCT

THU
02
NOV

MON
30
OCT

v/c 4:36ᵃᵐ
→ ♊ 8:08ᵃᵐ

FRI
03
NOV

v/c 8:28ᵖᵐ

Hallows' Eve/Samhain

TUE
31
OCT

SAT
04
NOV

→ ♌ 12:21ᵃᵐ

Saturn direct

Pacific Daylight Time (PDT) becomes Pacific Standard Time (PST)

EARTH
Send roots into Earth.
Find strength in the gifts you
have already received.

*What makes me grateful to be
alive at this time on Earth is . . .*

_____

_____

{REAP}

Daylight Saving Time ends

SUN
05
NOV

v/c 11:25ᵖᵐ

THU
09
NOV

→ ♎12:08ᵃᵐ

Mercury → Sagittarius

MON
06
NOV

→ ♍11:39ᵃᵐ

FRI
10
NOV

Election Day

TUE
07
NOV

SAT
11
NOV

New Moon Café

v/c 7:05ᵃᵐ
→ ♏10:39ᵃᵐ

WED
08
NOV

v/c 8:55ᵖᵐ

SUN
12
NOV

Venus → Libra

Obeying his conscience, a soldier resists orders.

STANDING
{TWELFTH MOON}
SCORPIO

I N THE DREAM OF THE STANDING MOON, *we bend our hands to the great task – ecologists, policy makers, and herb-witches alike – listening and tending the river's heart.*

A cloud of city enforcers descends like so many crows, scolding and harping. We are bustled away from our good green work.

But then a flash in our chest and something bright at the edges. Our coat of arms, our earthling mark, visibly pulses and glows. We cannot ignore our wildling oath.

Each of us alone must choose.

And will some remain and others step back? And do our tactics shift in accordance with conscience?

**Yes. Your authority flows from
the dream of Earth.**

What values-driven choice do you feel is at hand?

Identify a revolutionary act of love – in history or present time. How can it liberate you?

your guiding question for the month

write/draw/collage your ally here

For eons, human systems have risen, fallen, and completely transformed by effect of a single dissenting voice. Your inner compass is the authority here.

If your moral authority feels tested, follow your earthling heart. Remain in right relationship with the web of life, even if it means breaking old agreements. You can face challenges with the armor of integrity and purpose.

Cocoon weaver and wilderness guide Bill Plotkin defines soul as a person's unique eco-niche. This definition acknowledges that we are each a part of the whole. Enact your sacred vow to co-create the dream of Earth.

Make an offering ❀ Consult the oracle ❀ Build a paper shrine

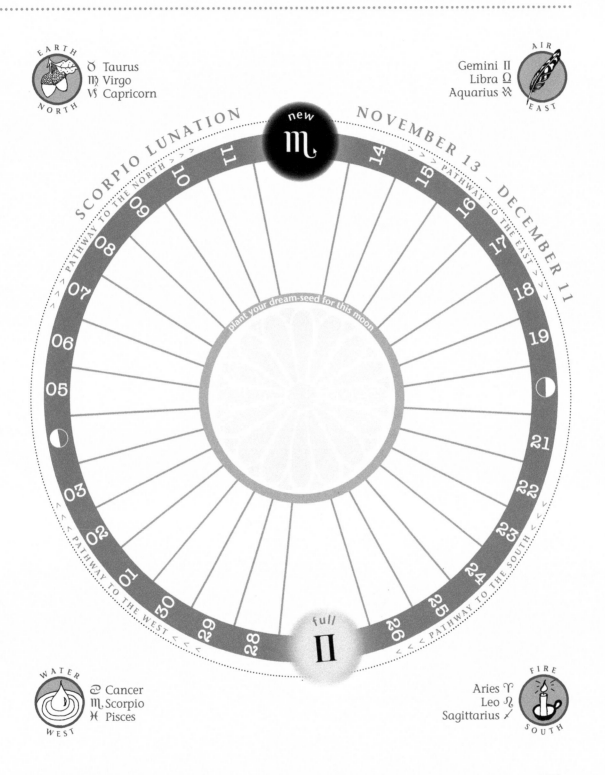

EARTH
NORTH
♉ Taurus
♍ Virgo
♑ Capricorn

AIR
EAST
Gemini ♊
Libra ♎
Aquarius ♒

SCORPIO LUNATION
NOVEMBER 13 – DECEMBER 11

PATHWAY TO THE NORTH >>>
PATHWAY TO THE EAST >>>

new
♏

11
10
09
08
07
06
05
03
02
01
30
29
28

14
15
16
17
18
19
21
22
23
24
25
26

plant your dream-seed for this moon

full
♊

PATHWAY TO THE WEST <<<
PATHWAY TO THE SOUTH <<<

WATER
WEST
♋ Cancer
♏ Scorpio
♓ Pisces

FIRE
SOUTH
Aries ♈
Leo ♌
Sagittarius ♐

{ENVISION}

A I R

Shift your perception. Realize you are an inseparable part of this Earth.

Knowing that the Earth is breathing through me, I am inspired to . . .

_____

_____

MON
13
NOV

♏

new
20°44′1:27ᵃᵐ
v/c 3:03ᵖᵐ
→⚹ 6:23ᵖᵐ

THU
16
NOV

TUE
14
NOV

FRI
17
NOV

WED
15
NOV

v/c 2:57ᵖᵐ
→♑ 11:41ᵖᵐ

SAT
18
NOV

v/c 12:27ᵃᵐ
→♒ 3:28ᵃᵐ

SUN
19
NOV

All listed times are Pacific Standard Time (PST)

FIRE

Step forward. This is your giveaway. Become generous with the world.

So that the world may flourish, I am willing to . . .

_____

_____

{ENRICH}

MON
20
NOV

v/c 2:50ᵃᵐ
→♓6:29ᵃᵐ

FRI
24
NOV

v/c 9:40ᵃᵐ
→♉12:29ᵖᵐ

Mars → Sagittarius

TUE
21
NOV

SAT
25
NOV

WED
22
NOV

v/c 7:10ᵃᵐ
→♈9:19ᵃᵐ

Sun → Sagittarius

SUN
26
NOV

v/c 1:52ᵖᵐ
→♊4:40ᵖᵐ

THU
23
NOV

Practice gratitude.

{SENSE}

WATER

Honor your love and your grief for the world. Create space for your feelings.

What is difficult to witness at this time is . . .

_____
_____

MON
27
NOV

Ⅱ

full
4°51' 1:16ᵃᵐ

THU
30
NOV

TUE
28
NOV

v/c 5:03ᵖᵐ
→ ♋10:54ᵖᵐ

FRI
01
DEC

v/c 5:07ᵃᵐ
→ ♌8:00ᵃᵐ

Mercury → Capricorn

WED
29
NOV

SAT
02
DEC

*"We must take our time and slow down.
We must rest and be mindful of
the power of our imagination.
The future is now."*

~ Tricia Hersey

SUN
03
DEC

v/c 6:11ᵖᵐ
→ ♍7:50ᵖᵐ

All listed times are Pacific Standard Time (PST)

EARTH

Send roots into Earth.
Find strength in the gifts you
have already received.

*What makes me grateful to be
alive at this time on Earth is . . .*

_____

_____

{REAP}

MON
04
DEC

Venus → Scorpio

TUE
05
DEC

WED
06
DEC

v/c 5:50ᵃᵐ
→ ♌8:35ᵃᵐ

Neptune direct

THU
07
DEC

FRI
08
DEC

v/c 5:05ᵖᵐ
→ ♏7:35ᵖᵐ

New Moon Café

SAT
09
DEC

SUN
10
DEC

MON
11
DEC

v/c 12:57ᵃᵐ
→ ♐3:11ᵃᵐ

A CHILD AND A DOG WEARING BORROWED EYEGLASSES.

ENACTMENT
{ THIRTEENTH MOON }
SAGITTARIUS

Give the

vision

away.

I N THE DREAM OF THE ENACTMENT MOON, *we are joined by the many. Bioneers, imagineers, enchantivists and earthlings all stand together.*

With jovial company, with honey and bread, we weave the tale of once-estranged humans come into radical belonging with earth. We share into the night as our lids grow heavy with reverie.

Our animal kin draw near, their eyes aglow with mischief. Their parting act of wild magic wafts into our midst.

And do we wake with eyes all 'round the body? And are these the eyes of belonging?

By your courage, my love,
The world is made new.

*What aspiration
are you playing at?
Feed the magic by
acting "as if".*

*Is there a point
of view it's time to
swap or try on?*

your guiding question for the month

write/draw/collage your ally here

The year is winding down, and you may want to transition into your new Dreamfruit 2024 for this lunar cycle. But before you go, take some time to review all that you've discovered on your journey through this year.

Visit your Mandala of Belonging on pg 16 to see the circle of care that has gathered around you. Reflect on your Notes from the Field to cull any medicine meant for you.

When you are ready, turn to Closing the Gate on pg 148 to uncover your personal fruits for the year.

Make an offering ✿ Consult the oracle ✿ Build a paper shrine

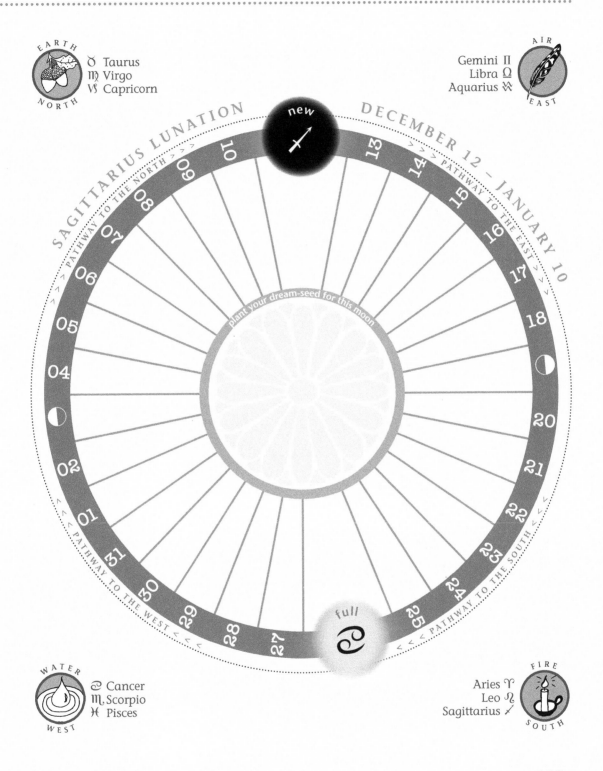

{ENVISION}

A I R

Shift your perception. Realize you are an inseparable part of this Earth.

Knowing that the Earth is breathing through me, I am inspired to . . .

_____

_____

_____

TUE
12
DEC

new
20°40' 3:32ᵖᵐ
v/c 10:48ᵖᵐ

Mercury retrograde

WED
13
DEC

→♑7:31ᵃᵐ

THU
14
DEC

FRI
15
DEC

v/c 8:04ᵃᵐ
→♒9:56ᵃᵐ

SAT
16
DEC

SUN
17
DEC

v/c 4:04ᵃᵐ
→♓11:58ᵃᵐ

"Suddenly this dream you are having matches everyone's dream, and the result is the world."

~ William Stafford

MON
18
DEC

All listed times are Pacific Standard Time (PST)

FIRE

Step forward. This is your giveaway. Become generous with the world.

So that the world may flourish, I am willing to . . .

_____

_____

{ENRICH}

TUE
19
DEC

v/c 1:03ᵖᵐ
→♈2:47ᵖᵐ

SAT
23
DEC

v/c 10:40ᵖᵐ

WED
20
DEC

SUN
24
DEC

→♊12:15ᵃᵐ

Winter Solstice

THU
21
DEC

v/c 6:47ᵖᵐ
→♉6:50ᵖᵐ

Sun → Capricorn

Practice kindness.

MON
25
DEC

v/c 11:55ᵖᵐ

FRI
22
DEC

Mercury → Sagittarius

{SENSE}

WATER

Honor your love and your grief for the world. Create space for your feelings.

What is difficult to witness at this time is . . .

_____

_____

TUE
26
DEC

→ ♋ 7:15ᵃᵐ
full
4°58' 4:33ᵖᵐ

Chiron direct

WED
27
DEC

THU
28
DEC

v/c 2:57ᵖᵐ
→ ♌ 4:23ᵖᵐ

FRI
29
DEC

Venus → Sagittarius

SAT
30
DEC

v/c 9:18ᵖᵐ

Jupiter direct

SUN
31
DEC

→ ♍ 3:53ᵃᵐ

MON
01
JAN

Begin again.

Mercury direct

TUE
02
JAN

→ ♎

All listed times are Pacific Standard Time (PST)

EARTH

Send roots into Earth.
Find strength in the gifts you
have already received.

*What makes me grateful to be
alive at this time on Earth is . . .*

_____

_____

{REAP}

WED
03
JAN

THU
04
JAN

Mars → Capricorn

FRI
05
JAN
→ ♏

New Moon Café

SAT
06
JAN

SUN
07
JAN
→

MON
08
JAN

TUE
09
JAN
→ ♑

WED
10
JAN

"There is nothing new under the sun, but there are new suns."

~ Octavia E. Butler

Closing the Gate

Thank you for traveling through the landscape of **Dreamfruit 2023**. The year is closing as our Sun rounds the corner to begin a new solar cycle. Take a moment to look back on your path and gather the fruits of your journey to carry into the year ahead . . .

. . . *We return to the misty shoreline where the scarlet-robed women have been listening all year. They have been here with their bare feet tracing patterns in the sand, translating your steps into shape and song. Step closer and see the design their path makes in the cool damp sand.*

One by one, they gather in circle around you. Thirteen of them side by side.

They see you. They have heard you crying and laughing as the moons grew and waned. They have divined wisps of your dreams as through a sea glass window. They each hold a verse to share about your journey, that only you can hear. If you're willing, ask them a question and let their answer be written across the threshold of the gate. ❧

WHAT FRUITS ARE WAITING FOR YOU AT THE GATE?

Illustration: Dan Reed Miller

Compendium for the Curious

In the pages ahead you will find a trove of keys, maps, and resources to support your Dreamfruit journey, including:

- **About Dream Logic and Creative Play** invites your deep imagination into practical expression.

- **Degree Symbols and the Sky Story** gives a basic orientation to the symbolic map of the year.

- **About the Moon** introduces our grandmother moon and some of the etiquette we can approach her with.

- **The Living Circle: Elements of Life** provides a magical introduction to the elements of Air, Fire, Water, Earth and Ether at the foundation of the world.

- **The Great Turning through the Zodiac** introduces the archetypal intelligence of the astrological signs and offers questions to guide us toward a regenerative future.

- **On Behalf of the Future: the Moon in Context** offers specific suggestions for further learning and action, aligned with the themes of each of this year's moons.

- The **Glossary of Terms, Assumptions, and Norms** defines and expounds upon the principles that weave throughout the landscape of Dreamfruit.

- **Resources and suggestions** for deepening your understanding of our social and planetary challenges, community solutions, and more.

Picture a vast sparkling web. Watch as one strand quivers when touched by a drop of rain. You'll then see the entire web come to life as the vibrating strand transmits its signal to the whole. Now imagine that this shimmering web is the whole of the cosmos.

Even within the limits of our modern imagination, we can stitch together what remains of the wild tongue with a genuine love for the world. It's then that the power of the deep imagination is initiated. The web starts to vibrate, and it shakes us from the trance of estrangement into what ecospiritual scholar, Thomas Berry, called the dream of Earth.

About Dream Logic

What is the shared language between Earth and Earthling? How can we be in conversation with the very matrix we're woven into?

The language of dreams speaks to something weirder than the modern mind is accustomed to. As such, this language can bypass the rational gatekeepers that tell us what is possible and what is not. As any corporate brand designer will tell you, far more information can be compressed into a single image than our linear minds can immediately grasp. The brief rituals and monthly vignettes of Dreamfruit are richly infused packets of information designed to activate the nonlinear mind and strengthen your capacity to imagine in a generative way.

Dream logic unlocks a hidden intelligence that can be tapped for insight and guidance. Within the world of Dreamfruit, we engage these images in a way that divines a path through the intensity of our Earth-moment and guides us toward the regenerative future that our earthling hearts and Gaia herself long for.

About Creative Play

Bear in mind the meta-context of our moment — the living Earth has been imperiled, and our creative nature is rising up. Dreamfruit wants to awaken your creative nature because that part of you fulfills a unique role in the spiritual ecology of the world.

By definition, creativity brings new possibilities into being. What better time than now to cultivate a playful and curious mind, nimble enough to envision new patterns and pathways toward something better?

All of the elements you find sprinkled throughout this almanac are offered in the open spirit of play and invitation. You're enthusiastically encouraged to play to your level, co-create with the pages, and let this almanac become what you most need along the way.

We each have our own ways of being with dreamtime. Techniques and symbolic associations are as wildly diverse as we are. Explore methods that help you be with the dream's mystery rather than force meaning from it. As you wind your way through the land of Dreamfruit, do what works for you, which may change over time.

Dreams give us cues from the deep imagination that guide us toward life-sustaining actions in our day-to-day lives.

 On the night of the New Moon read the Dream and Weave for that lunation. Highlight or underline images or phrases that stay with you. Let those images travel with you through the terrain of the month. Track insights and synchronicities as they arise, and note them in the dated calendar pages.

 As you consider the month's themes, is there a particular figure who could be a traveling companion through the terrain ahead? Using the "ally circle" provided, write, glue, or draw that companion into the circle. Play with lines, curves and color, letting your own delight and intuition take the lead. You are bringing your ally into focus for the coming month.

There exists among the wild children of Earth an ancient practice of attuning to the Great Circle and gathering messages from its many degrees. These messages are conveyed in images, dreams, and stories, received by us through the deep imagination.

As we connect with the organic flow of natural time, shifting attention from the grid of the Gregorian calendar, we can begin to sense these stories and images at play.

Degree Symbols & the Sky Story

The Dreamfruit journey is shaped by many modes of knowing. Aside from the languages of Nature, divination and dream, monthly themes are partly informed by the language of astrological degree symbols, specifically a system known as the Sabian symbols. These are a collection of 360 phrases that correlate to each degree of the zodiac.

After years of studying degree symbols, their remarkable resonance to the pattern and imprint of each new moon is unmistakable. Telling the story of the year through the images in these phrases reveals a dreamscape that we can enter with lucidity and intention. When you read each month's dream message in Dreamfruit, you are tuning in to the voice of the cosmos, as transmitted and translated through these symbols.

All of creation is dreaming and transmitting to itself all the time. Throughout the ages, witches, herbalists, and dream-tenders have traversed the communication lines between nature and psyche. By way of a few magical technologies — dream, image, and story — we can rest our own bodies alongside the dreaming body of Earth and, if luck is close by, hear her strange reverie. The Dreamfruit story has these magical technologies at its core.

Refer to the astrological wheel on the facing page to see which degrees will be activated by the new moons of 2023. Each year, the moon's cycles begin at a different degree of each sign.

Reading the chart of New Moon Sabian Symbols

Start with the earliest date on the wheel (the first new moon of the year) and trace the moon's path through each sign's constellation. Read along as each lunation adds its chapter to the story of the year, collecting dream images like pearls on a string.

As mentioned, the phrases included here are the Sabian symbols associated with that particular sign's degree. You can learn much more about the Sabians and how these symbols came about by visiting www.sabian.org/sabiansymbols.php.

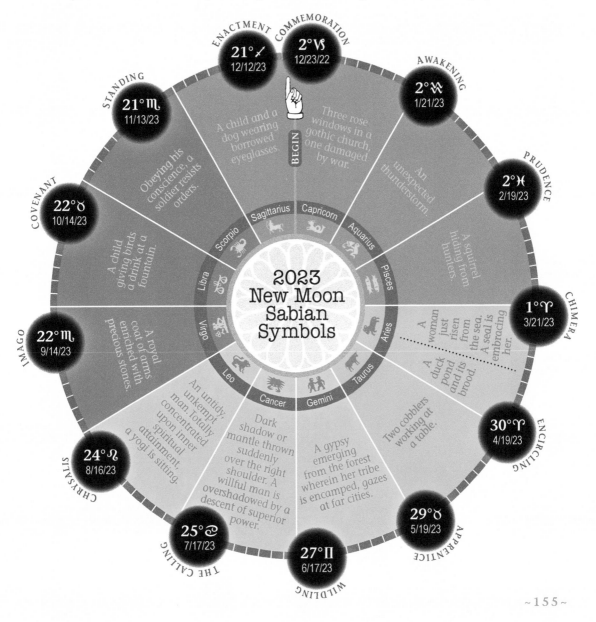

There is much to learn from Luna's monthly path. This section provides a rich exploration of the moon through the phases, signs, and elements.

Bear in mind that there is no fixed "meaning" of the moon as it travels through the sky. Use this information as a laboratory for your imagination. How does your experience and the quality of energy shift within and around you as the moon follows its path?

About the Moon

The cosmos is filled with strange wonders, not the least of which is our watery planet Earth and companion moon, Luna. The moon is our most proximate emissary of the night sky and, as such, one of the greatest gifts Luna offers to earth-dwellers is its role as a gateway to wonder.

Lunar Gifts

In 1972, the Apollo 17 lunar mission brought back a picture of planet Earth. Known as the Blue Marble photograph, this picture is the most reproduced image in the world and continues to have a profound impact on the human psyche. In this photograph we see ourselves as the moon has always seen us: whole. Luna, therefore, teaches us about witnessing.

Over millenia, the resonance between our bodies and the moon's body has grown and shaped our experience of natural cycles of time. The direct experience of lunar rhythms — through tides, menstrual cycles, light changes and more — reminds us that invisible forces have the power to change us. Luna teaches us about flow and unseen influences.

The modern mind is challenged to sense this connection with the beyond-human world. We've come to think of objects and other life forms as separate and inert. This worldview places humans at the center of things, opening the way to callous and rampant extraction of so-called "resources" rather than sensing our interrelatedness. Even a slight perceptual shift can reveal Creation as conscious and sentient, in companionship with itself. Slowing our pace and softening our gaze unveils the unique intelligence of other creatures, clouds, objects, rivers, mountains, and yes, the Moon. The moon is one of our earliest and most enduring relatives. Luna teaches us about kinship.

Lunar Etiquette

When we carry this animistic sense of the cosmos, a pathway opens to relatedness and mutual care for all that breathes with and through us. Etiquette grows from this kind of empathy.

Consider the moon as a living presence, a grandmother who has watched over our ancestors and witnessed life evolve on Earth. Luna shows us what we easily forget to see — night vision, dreams, and the steady tide of change. This grandmother is a companion, an elder, and a guide. Above all, we greet her not as a symbol or an abstraction, but as a conscious, sovereign presence with her own power and vulnerabilities.

Technological advances continue to project humans and our tools into space, while simultaneously inserting ever greater distance between the imagination and the cosmos. Space travel has quickly become an entertainment for the wealthy, even as our view of the night sky dwindles beneath a blanket of light pollution and extreme satellite coverage. Meanwhile space programs race toward a permanent mining presence on the lunar surface. We have not even begun to understand the effects of space debris and colonization on the great sky story, let alone the impact of diminished night sky visibility on the human psyche.

May you be inspired to advocate and act in kinship with our beloved Luna, sovereign companion and sky teacher.

 As we draw guidance and insight from the moon, it is important to reciprocate and act on her behalf. In 2021, a Declaration for the Rights of the Moon was drafted and is beginning to gain traction. You can register your support of this declaration at www.earthlaws.org.au.

Good moon habits grow over a lifetime. They can show up as lunar musings, moon walks, sky gazing and other magical acts. Give yourself plenty of time each month to cultivate a personal connection with Luna.

Cycles of Time: the Moon's Phases

NEW MOON

Begin in the quiet of the underground with the moist soil and the sleeping seed. When Luna begins her cycle, she is deeply rooted in her truest nature. Nobody can see her, and so her first steps and the direction she chooses are hers and hers alone.

WAXING CRESCENT MOON

Feel the quickening in the tendrils below the surface. Energy is gathering and Luna can be seen as a delicate crescent just above the setting sun. Her path is made clear and she gingerly steps with bare feet and fresh eyes.

FIRST QUARTER MOON

Both feet are firmly on course by the time Luna meets this balance point of first quarter. She stabilizes her foundation and grows in confidence. Good timing, because now the world is able to witness her chosen path.

WAXING GIBBOUS MOON

New growth spirals up from the nourishing soil. Our beloved moon gains momentum and her fullness feels inevitable. She collects and transforms sunlight into a force of its own and begins to pull on the waters of the world. Her crowning influence rises deep within us and this is true also of your own chosen path. Fruition is inevitable.

◯ FULL MOON

Who can sleep? Luna shines in her full glory and creates a "second day" after the Sun leaves its post. Feel your heart spread wide like petals and leaves. What you have planted and fed is all over you. Get a good look at the implications of its fruition, for better or for worse. Enjoy the moment and take good notes.

🌖 WANING GIBBOUS MOON

Wayward limbs push from awkward angles. Luna is suspended in the afterglow and there is a hint of realization dawning. Fill in the outlines as you reflect on and celebrate what has been accomplished.

🌗 THIRD QUARTER MOON

Returning to equipoise but now with arms laden, Luna carries the harvest of her accumulated experience and begins to discern what she must leave behind. Feel the spongy dark earth underfoot and turn firmly toward completion.

🌘 WANING CRESCENT MOON

She makes an altar in a secret place as her eyes begin to close. A crone's crescent can be seen in the early hours of dawn, and yet even now she works at trimming away the dross. Only what is essential remains. She sings the story of her journey even as her face turns toward the night.

🌑 DARK MOON

A wise one moves slowly across the water's edge. Her story is carefully stitched into her cloak as she finds shelter and stillpoint in the crags and caves of the coastline. Here she waits, dreams, and divines in the dark, rolling a grain of sand between her fingers.

The direct experience of lunar rhythms reminds us that invisible forces have the power to change us. Luna teaches us about flow and unseen influences.

 You're invited to visit www.Dreamfruit.world, where you can download a simple ceremonial outline to support your moon-magic journey.

The basic elements of Air, Fire, Water, and Earth form a living circle that shifts and shimmers as the moon traces her path through them.

As a spiritual practice, many earthlings cast a circle between the worlds by inviting these forces to gather near their respective Gates — with Nature below and Cosmos above, and the always abiding Mystery at the center.

The need for etiquette and an animistic sensibility applies as much to the realm of elemental intelligence as to our relationship with the moon herself. In this sacred circle, everyone breathes and listens together.

There are countless maps of meaning and elemental correspondences humans have conjured around the world. Those described here are particular to my tradition.

The Living Circle: Elements of Life

AIR

Gemini, Libra, Aquarius

Following the cycle of breath from the beginning of the inhale to the bottom of the exhale teaches us about time and flow. Life on Earth begins and ends with the breath.

Air's dual nature is inherently unitive even as it discerns and dissipates, making it sympathetic to the archetype of the Trickster.

Opening the East Gate, the winds of the world breathe with and through us. Feel the rush of life enter your lungs.

FIRE

Aries, Leo, Sagittarius

Feel the quickening of your pulse and the tingle in your nervous system. This is the spark of life flickering through you.

As a wild companion to humans for eons, Fire has earned our respect. As a literal agent of transformation, Fire holds the powers of creation and destruction in its fingertips.

When we are alert to this presence at the South Gate, life force rises through us to meet it. We still have much to learn from this force of nature, and so we greet it with playful ferocity to indicate that we are up to the task.

WATER

Cancer, Scorpio, Pisces

Early life took shape in the waters of the world. Our own bodies developed in the fluid space of the womb. Water teaches us about the great unconscious, the dreaming body, and the knowing beneath the knowing.

We ask the waters of the West Gate to carry our dreams and our grief, to dissolve and redistribute blockages, to transmute the energy in our emotional bodies through tears and laughter.

In times of sorrow, uncertainty, or fear, we seek out bodies of water. It is indeed life, and it is a sovereign intelligence that we are blessed to call kin.

EARTH

Taurus, Virgo, Capricorn

 Skin and bone, soil and stone. The material world resonates with the element of Earth, found at the North Gate. The human body's skeletal scaffolding is our most proximate reminder of this elemental guide. The soil beneath our feet holds the stories and ash of our ancestors, and nourishes our bodies through the foods that grow from it.

We return to Earth at the end of each day, where we are reminded of limitation as well as abundance. Practical concerns are addressed here at the North Gate.

SPACE/ETHER

Void of Course

 After the moon makes its final planetary aspect, and before entering a new sign, it is said to be void of course. It is in the "between."

Pause now and release your eyes into the room you're in. Rather than directing your gaze toward the objects around you, trick your eyes into seeing the space between them. Perceive the negative space and notice how it determines and supports everything else.

The circle completes itself here at the Center Gate, home of the Great Mystery. Although it is unseen, the space that resides at the heart of all things holds tremendous power.

The prevailing wisdom is that when the moon is void of course, it is not advised to attempt magical workings.

 Trace the moon's path through the elements by noticing which sign it is passing through day by day (this information is found on the daily calendar pages). You can color code the days on the Moon Wheels each month to track the elemental energies as they shift.

Among the many maps humans have created to make meaning of our universe is the astrological zodiac. The western system includes twelve signs, each one overseen by an archetypal presence.

These archetypes can be powerful teachers, asking us to remember and reciprocate the gift and glory of life. Each one of them poses a question as the moon passes through its domain.

The questions offered here arise from healing intent, aimed at fortifying you for the Great Turning — turning from a depleted world of toxic individualism toward a regenerative future where all life thrives.

The Great Turning through the Zodiac

♈ ARIES

Watch for an initiating spark. Luna becomes a dignified warrior when she stands in this fire sign. Fresh energy is available to be channeled in a life-giving direction. What awakens a fierce and revolutionary love within you?

♉ TAURUS

Remember that we all must rest and that pleasure can be a wise teacher. When Luna passes through this earthy domain, allow yourself to pause and to make room for tending your needs and cultivating resources. Create something beautiful for Nature — a project, an altar, a garden.

♊ GEMINI

Allow curiosity to grow into wonder. Ask better questions and listen to learn. Reconsider your perspective and examine the data. What helps you shake free from narrow certitude?

♋ CANCER

Luna's home sign, she is reflective and nourishing, bringing her devotion and care to all within reach. How do you protect what you love? Name who and what you love.

♌ LEO

Feel your heart pump blood through your body. This is where Luna can be found as she moves through the sign of Leo. Let her playful side come through, but watch for the invisible line where play becomes drama. How do you most want to show up at this dire moment on Earth? What story would you be most proud to tell your great great grandchildren?

♍ VIRGO

Service and preparation come to the foreground. Take some private time to assess and analyze where your energies are best expended. If there are pulls on your attention, step back to discern whether they are contributing or distracting. What is truly yours to do?

♎ LIBRA

Pause for a calming breath. Maybe two. Luna carries herself with a cool bearing through this breezy realm. Consider all sides of an issue and ask, what does Justice ask of each of us in this moment?

♏ SCORPIO

Denial is not a strategy. Dodging the intense emotions that are baked into this challenging earth-time will only prolong and exacerbate the situation. Yes, Luna keeps it real in this deep sign. What truth is pressing on your heart, demanding expression?

♐ SAGITTARIUS

Our beloved Luna grows expansive and inspired when she visits the archetypal Archer. What encourages you when your optimism flags? Time outdoors with the natural world will strengthen your spirit.

♑ CAPRICORN

Look to the mountains for perspective on time. Luna has witnessed epochal changes on Earth, the evolution of humankind, the stories of our ancestors. It takes patience and effort to build the structures and core systems that will endure. What are you willing to work for?

♒ AQUARIUS

Sometimes flipping the script will return the story to its true purpose. In this piercing air sign, Luna is likely to cut through any nonsense with striking insights on behalf of the greater good. What is your upgraded vision for the whole community of life?

♓ PISCES

Our dear reflective Luna is at home in the easy flow of Pisces. See how she relaxes and lets go. There is much to gain through surrender, not the least of which is access to inner wisdom. What does your healing heart tell you is needed at this time?

 As the moon moves through each of the signs, notice what you notice. You are your own best laboratory for tracing the moon's influence. You can "read the day" by combining the passages about the moon's current sign, element, and phase.

Dreamfruit was created to support greater intimacy with the planet. There has never been a more perfect moment to remember that human activity doesn't take place in a vacuum.

This list of "mundane" monthly suggestions is here to draw your attention to the ecological challenges of our time. As your biophilia deepens, the plans and magic you make from month to month will become more informed by the context we all share.

On Behalf of the Future: the Moon in Context

1st Moon: Commemoration
Learn about personal and collective trauma and its impact on our world. Host a watch party and discussion of the documentary, *The Wisdom of Trauma*.

2nd Moon: Awakening
Prepare your "go-bag" to have on hand for an emergency. Find a list of suggested supplies and information particular to your community at https://www.ready.gov/.

3rd Moon: Prudence
Find ways that warriorship can be harnessed to protect the flourishing of life. What if hunters took a pledge of guardianship? Discover the Akashinga: the Brave Ones at https://www.iapf.org/.

4th Moon: Chimera
Learn about ecofeminism and the measurable improvement in ecological health when women have access to education, healthcare, and civic power. Read *Dreaming the Dark* by Starhawk.

5th Moon: Encircling
Embrace simplicity as a counterpoint to the speed and complex demands of the modern world. Learn about the Great Simplification at www.thegreatsimplification.com/animations

6th Moon: Apprentice
Identify one lost art of homesteading that you can hone or teach as a skill.

7th Moon: Wildling
Learn about traditional ecological knowledge and how it can lead the way to climate resilience. Visit www.indigenousclimateaction.com/

8th Moon: The Calling
Read Sharon Blackie's essay about the eco-heroine's journey at www.jungplatform.com/article/the-eco-heroines-journey.

9th Moon: Chrysalis
Support contemporary nature-based rites of passage. Consider participating in a wilderness fast. Visit www.SchoolofLostBorders.org.

10th Moon: Imago
Identify the pivotal moments in humankind's evolutionary journey. Trace human evolution at least as far as our watery origins. Visit www.journeyoftheuniverse.org/.

11th Moon: Covenant
Learn about and support the Migratory Bird Protection Act. https://defenders.org/protecting-migratory-birds

12th Moon: Standing
Consider the moral authority required to intervene in Business as Usual. Organize a watch party for the documentary *Awake: A Dream from Standing Rock.*

13th Moon: Enactment
Visit and amplify the NotTooLateClimate.com website for a shift in perspective. There are earthlings doing good green works!

"In the face of impermanence and death, it takes courage to love the things of this world and to believe that praising them is our noblest calling."

~ Joanna Macy

Glossary of Terms, Assumptions & Norms

Cultural norms and assumptions alive within Dreamfruit are herein defined, clarified, or gently expounded upon. Collected from our ancestors, guides, and friends, here we animate the principles of Dreamfruit's landscape of transformation.

Allies. The beings, supports, and friends with whom we share a common purpose. Allies may be visible or invisible to the eye. The bond is brief or enduring, depending on the mutual agreement. Allies can be creatures, plants, words, images, or other unexpected guides who bring their own magic to the task at hand.

Animism. A view of the world as conscious and sentient, bringing a sense of the natural intelligence and companionship of nonhuman presences. The perception of a unique spiritual essence within creatures, objects, words, planets, rivers, mountains, and clouds.

Almanac. A friendly reference book composed of lists, tables, and brief articles relating to a particular area of interest. A yearly calendar showing the movement of the sun, the changes of the moon, and other seasonal data.

Anima Mundi. The World Soul. An intrinsic connection between all living things on the planet. A web of interrelatedness that echoes the way the soul is connected to the human body. See also *The Weave*.

The Between. The liminal space between what was and what is not yet fully formed. Buddhist tradition calls this the bardo. In initiatory processes, the between is referred to as "threshold" time. In magical practices, casting a circle creates a space between worlds. What happens between the worlds happens in all the worlds.

Biophilia. A love of life and the living world. A strong emotional bond with nature and all living things. A felt sense of mutual existence.

Birthright tools and magical technologies. Earthlings have inherent skills, tools, and adaptations that can shape our inner and outer landscapes. These tools wait in a basket of woven gold, under the branches of the World Tree. Included are the imagination, the awakening heart, the language of symbols and imagery, somatic intelligence, dream states, storytelling, the language of stars, art and creative play, and co-creation with the living world. The basket's gifts are endless, and so it helps to experiment with unexpected and joyful means.

Business as Usual. When we find ourselves imagining a future not unlike the past, with the default social and economic settings still in place, then we are living in the illusion of Business as Usual. Another clue is a creeping sense of human supremacy and separateness from nature.
See also *The Stories at Play*.

The Context. Circumstances that may be beyond our personal sphere of influence, but nevertheless have a very real impact on our lives. The Context is collective and always changing. In 2023, it includes species loss, public health crises, supply shortages, climate breakdown, and the polarization of modern society. Good times.
See also *Industrial Growth Society*.

Deep Imagination. The human imagination is an extraordinary tool of creation. When we engage it with lucid intention, we can envision a regenerative future, and become participants in the dream of Earth. Nature speaks to us through the Deep Imagination. Our inherent and ancient land bond can help to restore this information pathway.
See also *Sacred Attention*.

Deep Time. Most commonly refers to geologic time. In Dreamfruit, Deep Time also indicates a sense of Kairos, or the space between time. Entering Deep Time, we remember and gain access to our evolutionary heritage, our ancestors. We become sensitive to the great ribbon of time extending into the future, and can greet those beings who live there and will dream of us as their ancestors.

The Dream of Earth. A phrase offered by ecotheologian Thomas Berry, to conjure the interplay of consciousness within the web of life. A much better channel to direct our antennae toward.
See also *Gaia*.

Earthling. Dynamic reciprocity with all our relations is the innate human condition. We return to the circle of belonging by attuning to natural time, engaging the deep imagination, and seeing sentience in the nonhuman world. We then embrace the indelible truth that we are woven into the fiber of Earth's body. Each earthling is called to fulfill their unique eco-niche as part of the planetary organism.
See also *Sacred Assignment*.

Gaia. The mother goddess of all life on Earth. Also, the planet Earth herself as a complex, interacting, and self-regulating single living being.

The Great Turning. One of the Stories at Play, this term was first used by Craig Schindler and Gary Lapid and popularized by Joanna Macy. She describes it as "a name for the essential adventure of our time: the shift from the Industrial Growth Society to a life-sustaining civilization."
See also *The Stories at Play*.

Industrial Growth Society. Chronic and pathological extraction of materials from nature in order to prop up what youth activist Greta Thunberg calls the "fairy tale of endless growth"; an inherently unsustainable and system-wide virus of separation and dominance. See also *The Context*.

Metamorphosis. Eco-depth psychologist Bill Plotkin offers this as a metaphor for awakening to our mythopoetic identity. The journey of transformation passes through several stages, including the chrysalis, dissolution, and imago. See also *Spiral of Reconnection*.

Radical Belonging. This profound sense of interrelatedness expands our identity to include all beings, giving value to humanity as members of a larger body. It arises by attuning to natural time, the deep imagination, and the animistic world. At the heart of Dreamfruit is the path away from the shadow of separation into radical belonging. See also *Earthling*.

Sacred Assignment. A fundamental code for human dignity and living in balance with all creation. While everyone is universally called to live in accord with a greater cosmic order, each of us is born with a manner of being and path unique to us. In Dreamfruit, your sacred assignment refers to what is yours to do, to be, and to tend. As a human Earth-being, you have a particular niche that, when fulfilled, brings greater wholeness to the world and allows life to flourish well beyond your life span.

Sacred Attention. Your mental and emotional sovereignty. On any given day, our minds and hearts are at risk of being hijacked by the sheer volume of information and fervent opinions that pour from our screens. It requires great care to act as the curator and authority of what informs your worldview. In popular terms, this is referred to as "decolonizing the mind." Tending sacred attention is a core Earthling practice.

Spiral of Reconnection. A path of sequenced practices within the Work that Reconnects that passes through four successive stages. The stages include: coming from gratitude, honoring our pain for the world, seeing with new eyes, and going forth. These stages inform the prompts for each elemental "moon week" in Dreamfruit.

The Stories at Play. The world is made of stories. Many of them are true at the same time, and some may be truer than others. As sovereign beings, we can choose which story we feed with our attention and effort. On offer are, for example, the Story of Separation, the Great Turning, and the New Story. It could also be that we are living inside a Great Love Story, as we each awaken to our fundamental connection with all life. The dreams of Dreamfruit are written to feed the Great Love Story of now.

Trance of Estrangement. The illusion that humans are somehow not part of the body of Earth. Can result from collective or inherited trauma, profound grief at the harm caused to the Earth, despair over the climate crisis, or general numbing of empathy for the sentient world. Dreamfruit exists to support the healing of this illusion.
See also *Earthling.*

The Weave. The unbroken web of life that moves within, between, and through all things. When we slow down and listen, the Weave will surprise us with its benevolent wisdom and support. See also *Birthright Tools.*

The Work that Reconnects. A body of work based on the teachings of ecophilosopher Joanna Macy and practiced worldwide as a means of acknowledging our collective despair, awakening a sense of connection to the wider circle of life, and taking empowered action on its behalf.

"We are becoming the systems we need . . . we have to remember how to care for each other."

~ adrienne maree brown

Resources

Gifts from the Community

Tree Sisters is a reforestation project that inspires feminine nature-based leadership in changing the story of humans and nature.

The Nap Ministry reminds us that rest is a form of resistance to the Business as Usual story of urgency and dominance. www.TheNapMinistry.com

Animas Valley Institute offers nature-based initiatory experiences to open the door for humans to restore their bond with the wild soul. www.Animas.org

Work that Reconnects offers a crucial path to transform despair and overwhelm into connected and heartful action. Find workshops at www.workthatreconnects.org.

New Moon Café uses the Dreamfruit Almanac and deep imagination to animate the dream and themes for each month of the year. Sign up at www.Dreamfruit.world.

Stories We Tell Each Other

Broken Earth Trilogy by N. K. Jemisin, published by Orbit Books. A bracing epic that lays bare the emotional core of social injustice, earth magic, and human resilience.

Station Eleven by Emily St. John Mandel (2014). A layered and empathetic view of a post-pandemic world, and art's role in the reflowering of culture. Also a miniseries on HBOMax.

The Maya Greenwood series by Starhawk, published by Califia Press. The three-book series includes Walking to Mercury (1997), The Fifth Sacred Thing (1993), and City of Refuge (2016). Together these books provide practical and magical tactics for rebuilding a broken world.

Dandelion Trilogy by Rivera Sun, published by Rising Sun Press (2018). Disciplined nonviolence as a means of social transformation, set in the United States in more-or-less present time.

Promethea by Alan Moore published by America's Best Comics/Wildstorm (1999-2005) A graphic novel series invoking the power of magic and imagination to shape our world.

Earthseed Duology by Octavia E. Butler, published by Seven Stories Press. A prescient and frank series set in the 2020's that follows the birth of a new world amidst systemwide collapse.

Words, Sounds, and Pictures

Recordings and Websites

Dreamfruit Love 2023 playlist curated on Spotify throughout the year by Elizabeth Russell.

Global Sunrise: the Musical Sounds of Dawn recorded by Gordon Hempton

Songs from the Bardo by Laurie Anderson

NotTooLateClimate.com website from Rebecca Solnit

Resilience.org website from Post Carbon Institute

Podcasts

For the Wild podcast with Ayana Young

Living Myth podcast with Michael Meade

Octavia's Parables podcast with Toshi Reagon and adrienne maree brown

We as Nature podcast by Flourishing Diversity

What Could Possibly Go Right? podcast with Vicki Robin

Your Undivided Attention podcast with Tristan Harris, Center for Humane Technology

Documentary Film

America Outdoors PBS series (2022). A look at the wide spectrum of nature-love in the U.S. hosted with warmth and candor by Baratunde Thurston.

Fantastic Fungi directed by Louie Schwartzberg (2019). A consciousness-shifting film about the ecological magic and healing potential of mycelium.

Kiss the Ground by Josh and Rebecca Tickell of Big Picture Ranch (2020). Narrated by Woody Harrelson. An inspiring film that reveals a viable and accessible response to climate change.

The Social Dilemma by Jeff Orlowski (2020). Tech insiders with a conscience make clear the serious human impact of social media.

The Wisdom of Trauma by Science and Nonduality (SAND) with Gabor Maté (2021). Clarifies the connection between trauma and addiction, offering a vision of healing for the collective crises of modernity.

Things to Read

Inspiring and provocative books to consider, this is only a partial list of sources I've drawn from in creating this almanac. I hope this list provides a frame of reference as you explore the themes of Dreamfruit.

Berry, Thomas. *The Great Work: Our Way Into the Future.* New York: Three Rivers Press, 1999.

Hübl, Thomas. *Healing Collective Trauma: A Process for Integrating Our Intergenerational and Cultural Wounds.* Boulder: Sounds True, 2020.

Jamail, Dahr, and Stan Rushworth, eds. *We Are the Middle of Forever: Indigenous Voices from Turtle Island on the Changing Earth.* New York: The New Press, 2022.

Johnson, Ayana, and Katharine Wilkinson, eds. *All We Can Save: Truth, Courage, and Solutions for the Climate Crisis.* New York: One World, 2020.

Macy, Joanna, et al. *Thinking Like a Mountain: Towards a Council of All Beings.* Philadelphia: New Society Publishers, 1988.

Mitchell, Sherri. *Sacred Instructions: Indigenous Wisdom for Living Spirit-Based Change.* Berkeley: North Atlantic Books, 2018.

Plotkin, Bill. *The Journey of Soul Initiation: A Field Guide for Visionaries, Evolutionaries and Revolutionaries.* Novato: New World Library, 2021.

Russell, Elizabeth. *Dreamfruit: Interactive Almanac for Radical Belonging.* Eugene, OR: Earth Dragon Press, 2020-2022.

Production Credits:

Marcy Setniker — generous reflection and copy editing

Ted Owen — loving enhancements and epic graphic design support

Elise Crohn — generative dialogue and karmic collaboration

Beth Lorio — playful insights, video magic and moon-based illustrations

Aunia Kahn — vital soundboarding, photography and web design

Dreamfruit Travelers — curiosity, wonder, and willingness to play

Sabian Symbol Illustrations:

Beth Lorio makes art because she is a part of the creative consciousness of the Earth. Her two and three dimensional artwork as well as videography can be found at bethlorio.com.

Moon Phase Illustration:

Dan Reed Miller is a Cascadian artist, illustrator, writer, musician, and performer. He finds and follows a common thread of dynamic balance at the edge of improvisation and composition, chaos and order. Follow on Instagram: @danreedmiller and @medicine_tree_arts

❧ AN INVITATION ❧

New Moon Café

Join us online for monthly travelers' tips and deep imagination sessions.

1ST MOON: COMMEMORATION – *Dec. 22*

2ND MOON: AWAKENING – *January 21*

3RD MOON: PRUDENCE – *February 18*

4TH MOON: CHIMERA – *March 18*

5TH MOON: ENCIRCLING – *April 15*

6TH MOON: APPRENTICE – *May 20*

7TH MOON: WILDLING – *June 17*

8TH MOON: THE CALLING – *July 15*

9TH MOON: CHRYSALIS – *August 12*

10TH MOON: IMAGO – *September 9*

11TH MOON: COVENANT – *October 14*

12TH MOON: STANDING – *November 11*

13TH MOON: ENACTMENT – *December 9*

Dates are also listed in the monthly calendar pages.

Learn more at www.Dreamfruit.world

Loving Appreciation

I'm blessed with friendships that call me into my earthling nature. Thank you to the circles of women, creatives, and changemakers who walk, listen, and connect moon by moon, year by year. From this ground, the community response to our first ever crowdfunding campaign was inspiring and generous. Thank you for believing in and backing Dreamfruit 2023!

This year, a new form is bubbling up from the secret Dreamfruit cauldron, the beginnings of local book groups. Bright blessings and gratitude to the emerging cadre of tour guides setting their own community Dreamfruit circles into motion.

Astonishing gestures of love and talent poured into the production of this year's Dreamfruit. Great sparkle-ponies of appreciation prance in a circle around you, Aunia, Elise, Marcy, Beth, and Ted for holding my hand over the finish line.

It's no secret that 2022 was not my favorite year. It rode in carrying loss in its arms, and has left many things parched and wandering. But within its eyes and pockets, I have seen only love. Thank you, Mom, for the long view.

My beloved partner, intrepid in both foolish and wise endeavors, I offer oceans and skies of thanks for being the guardian of my writerly sanctuary and for joining in my antics.

P oet, witch, and joyful earthling **Elizabeth Russell** has apprenticed herself to the voice of nature for most of her life. Her work inspires us to reconnect with the intelligence of the living Earth by awakening our birthright powers of deep imagination.

With her Integrative Arts programs and the Dreamfruit series of almanacs, she has created an enchanted world that brings the Great Turning to life — in our imagination and daily lives.

Elizabeth lives in Oregon, where she feeds the birds, hosts moon-magic circles, and leads visionary experiments to inspire radical engagement with the living cosmos.

Visit online to join the *New Moon Café*, and connect with the Dreamfruit community. ❧

www.Dreamfruit.world

CPSIA information can be obtained
at www.ICGtesting.com
Printed in the USA
BVHW022327031122
650886BV00001B/1